SPIRITUAL
HEALTH
ENCOUNTERS

NANCY GOUDIE

First Edition 2016

ISBN 978-095645124-8

Concept design by Ray Goudie and Nancy Goudie
Graphic design by Lewis Royal
Photo by Dave Pratt

Published by New Generation Music,
Caedmon Complex,
Bristol Road,
Thornbury,
Bristol,
BS35 3JA,
UK

www.ngm.org.uk

Printed and bound in Great Britain by
TJ International Ltd, Padstow, Cornwall

I want to dedicate this book to the memory of Smith Wigglesworth (1859-1947), whose life story constantly inspires, encourages and challenges me to go deeper with God. He was a powerful man of God who not only preached about Jesus but also knew him intimately.

Contents

Recommendations for Spiritual Health Encounters

"A must read, Nancy's wisdom is both spiritual and experiential. She lives the truths of this book."
John Partington - National Leader, AOG GB

"I have known Nancy and her husband Ray since before they left their jobs to venture out and give all their time to serve the needs of others. What she has to say is drawn from a deep well of experience and out of the integrity of many years of giving sacrificially. This book is practical, accessible and fun to use!"
Graham Kendrick - Worship Leader

"Nancy's passion and skill in communicating her message of spiritual 'fitness' is evident to all who meet her. This book will help you exercise your faith muscles and tone up your heart for God. I thoroughly recommend it to you."
Rosemary Conley CBE - Author, Broadcaster and UK's Health and Fitness Guru

"Nancy Goudie has an infectious eagerness to know God better. This book communicates that enthusiasm. Read it and have your faith deepened."
Revd Canon J.John – Evangelist

"Nancy Goudie is an inspiration!"
Rob Parsons OBE - Author and Chairman of Care for the Family

"In this book Nancy has made true spirituality understandable and accessible. She and I have been great friends for a long time. I have watched her in the midst of unexpected joy and uncalled for sorrow and I know her strength lies in her wonderful friendship with Christ. As you read this book and follow her programmes you too will discover what an adventure it is to really know Jesus."
Sheila Walsh – Singer, Songwriter, Author and Speaker

"Nancy's commitment to Christ and her love for people is a shining testimony. Her unique programmes are radical and refreshing and the evidence of God's anointing is seen in changed lives. We wholeheartedly recommend this book."
Lyndon and Celia Bowring – Care Trust

"Nancy Goudie truly is a woman whose intimacy with her Heavenly Father shines through her daily communication and walk of faith. Only one who is truly rooted and grounded in him can exhibit abundant life, peace and courage as she does. You inspire us to go deeper Nancy!"
Ken and Lois Gott - Founders and Directors of House of Prayer Europe and President/CEO of Hopespring

"We live in times of despair and uncertainty in a chaotic world; but in the midst of all this Nancy has written a timely book about intimacy with God. It is in drawing close to God and spending time in His presence that we are able to restore and establish our hope, experience peace and live joyfully!"
Pastors Kofi and Jayne Banful – Praise Christian Centre, London

Acknowledgments

I am deeply grateful to the following people for the way they have helped me in the preparation of this book:

To **my incredible husband, Ray,** who encouraged me to write this edited and expanded version of this book. Without his insistence, I don't think this book would ever have seen the light of day. Ray, thank you that you have always been my best friend and greatest supporter. You have always believed in me.

To many of the **key ladies from my Spiritual Health Weekends** who told me they thought the publishing of this new book would be more than a good idea. You all know who you are but I'm not sure you understand how much your words and actions bless me. Thank you all for your many encouragements.

To **Sharon Cann** who proofread this book and then told me she enjoyed it so much that she was going to purchase a copy when it came out - what an encouragement. Thanks for your careful proof reading and for your amazing friendship Sharon.

To **Kat Bradford** who volunteered to check all the scriptures within the book – and there are many!! Thank you Kat - you are brilliant.

To **Jill Naismith** who spent hours going through the book for me before I sent it off to the printers. I was so encouraged when she told me the teaching challenged her as she read the book. Jill, you are such a blessing in so many ways.

To **Lewis Royal** who brought his wonderful creativity to the design and graphics of this book. Lewis – you are a great friend and a brilliant designer and it is always a huge delight to work with you.

To **Derek Tiffany, my pa** who constantly helps me in every big or small thing that needs to be done. Derek, I am so grateful for your help and for your friendship throughout the many years we have known you.

To **Zoe Wickham** who stands with Ray and myself in everything we do. She is always ready to help in any way she can whether practically or with her many encouragements. Zoe, you are truly amazing!

To **all who have written throughout the years** saying that these programmes and plans have changed their lives and that their relationship with Jesus has gone so much deeper. Woohoo – that is what the book is meant to do!

And finally, to my **Heavenly Father** whose love and faithfulness throughout the years overwhelms me. Thank you for the depths of your presence and for the hunger in my heart to know you more. My prayer is that you will use what you have given me in this book to bring many people into an even deeper and more intimate walk with you. Let us all experience your love and passion in ways that we have never known before.

Preface

"I'm so glad to meet you because you see I became a Christian through you." I was speaking at a church in Derbyshire, England, and during one of the breaks, a lady approached me and spoke the above words. She said, *"You won't know me, but I gave my life to the Lord Jesus through you. Can I tell you my story?"* I was intrigued so I sat down and listened to what was an amazing story. This lady told her husband one day that she had received a dream from God. In her dream, she saw a book. On the front cover of this book was a lady in fitness gear and as she looked at the book, she heard God said to her *'I want you to get a copy of this book and read it'*. Nothing like this had ever happened to her before so she found it quite bizarre! However, a few weeks later, she was in a library and saw my 'Spiritual Health Plan' book. When she saw it she said excitedly to her husband, *"This is the book! This is the book I saw in my dream!"*

She took a copy home and before she got to the third chapter, she had given her heart and life to the Lord Jesus. Sometime after that, while she was walking down a street in Derbyshire, she saw a poster in a shop window with my photo on it. She again said to her husband, *"That's the author of the book!"* She noticed that I was speaking at a local church on the Saturday. Her plans for that weekend had been cancelled twice so she was free to come along and tell me her amazing story. Isn't it great that God uses us even when we are unaware of what he is doing? There are so many other stories I've heard of how God has used my books, 'Developing Spiritual Wholeness', 'Spiritual Health Plan' and 'Spiritual Health Workout'. All these books are now out of print, but many people have been asking me to release them again and so I am very excited about releasing this book, which again gives people the opportunity to go deeper with God. I have updated and edited my Spiritual Health Workout book and have also written some brand new chapters and programmes.

My prayer is that as you read and 'do' this book, God will meet with you in a dynamic way and you will discover rich and incredible intimacy deep in the presence of God.

NANCY GOUDIE

1   Keeping Spiritually Fit

It was quite incredible. I'd never seen anything quite like it before. An en-suite bedroom with a double jacuzzi bath complete with cushions on either side! A number of years ago, close friends of ours invited my husband Ray, our son Daniel and myself to spend a holiday with them in the Lake District. They booked us into a wonderful hotel that had its own leisure facilities. When we arrived there, we couldn't believe our eyes. The bedroom was amazing, complete with its incredible bath.

The next day our friends, John and Rose Lancaster, together with their family, decided to go on a bike ride and asked Ray if he wanted to join them. Ray explained that he had not been on a bike for years and didn't have any of the right clothing for mountain biking. However, as they had brought extra clothing and a bike for him, he finally ran out of excuses. They said they would only take him on a short bike ride of eight miles. Ray's response was *"EIGHT MILES!"* They reassured him that although it sounded a lot of miles they would take it easy and he would be fine. As Daniel was only six at the time, I volunteered to stay behind and *suffer* in the luxury swimming pool and then meet them in a coffee shop when the bike ride was over!

I laughed when I saw Ray in his biking gear! My trendy husband was wearing what I called 'incontinent shorts' – shorts that had padding which help to make bike riding more comfortable! With my laughter ringing in his ears, off he went, a little shakily at first but soon he was cycling like he'd done it all his life. As he went down his first hill he thought to himself, *"This is going to be easy!"* If you have ever been to the Lake District in England, you will know that it is a very beautiful part of the country; however, a lot of its beauty is derived from the fact that it is quite mountainous.

Ray was doing well until he encountered his first mountain. His legs started to seize as he struggled up the hill. John, Rose and the rest of the cycling party zoomed up to the top of the hill, where they stopped and sympathetically waited for Ray. He eventually had to get off and *push* the bike the rest of the way up. Bikers kept passing him and, as you can imagine, he felt extremely embarrassed at being so unfit. When he got there, he discovered to his horror another hill just around the corner. What a nightmare!

Ray said there were times throughout the bike ride when he felt he was going to be sick. At other times he just wanted to lie down and die, or to cry because he felt so ill. On numerous occasions he felt like giving up. The only time he felt exhilarated was when he was going downhill! After what seemed like an eternity, Ray asked, *"How many more miles is it until we finish?"* He then discovered that they had actually got lost and were having to cycle the long way round and cross over some of the biggest mountains.

Meanwhile Daniel and I, after a leisurely swim, were sitting in a café waiting for the others to arrive. We were just contemplating chocolate cake and coffee when John, who had cycled on ahead, came in and asked me if I would go in the car to pick Ray up. He told me not to worry and said, *"We've done a few miles more than we had anticipated and Ray's completely exhausted."* When I picked Ray up in the car, he looked as though he couldn't move another muscle, although there was just a small hint of accomplishment etched on his face. I later discovered that he had cycled, walked and almost crawled twenty-four miles! Now I understood why we had a room with a jacuzzi bath!

GET FIT!

Ray's experience reflects what it's sometimes like in our Christian life. When it comes to problems in our lives, they can often seem like a big hill or even a mountain in front of us. How are we going to cope? How are we going to get over this problem? If Ray had been exercising regularly on a bike then the hills would not have seemed so much of a problem. All our friends zoomed to the top of the hill because they were fit and healthy. It may have taken more out of them than a smaller hill, but it wasn't nearly as difficult for them as it had been for Ray. I dread to think how I would have coped, if they had taken me!

Similarly, if we are exercising our spiritual life regularly then the problems and difficulties that we come across in life will not seem as hard. It's important to exercise physically, but so much more important to exercise spiritually. I have to say that even though Ray found this bike ride difficult, he wouldn't have missed it for the world and it gave us both a keen desire to go biking more regularly. Try exercising spiritually and it will give you a deeper desire to get to know God and will also affect those who are looking on!

WHY THIS BOOK?

It was back in 1985 when God first began to talk to us about revival being on his heart for Britain and many other nations of the world. One of the important things God told us was that we should prepare for what he was about to do in our nation. I am more convinced than ever that one of the preparations which is crucial to us all is the need to learn to walk in intimacy with God. Many people tell me of their desire to get closer to God and have their walk with God deepen, but they don't know how to do that. Quite a number of people ask me, *"How do you actually hear from God?"* This book will help to give you the answers to that type of question, but also it will give you the tools to know how to practically do that. I know that no matter where you are in your walk with God, whether you are a new Christian, or whether you have been a Christian for a long time, this book will help you to discover more intimacy with God. You will realise as you turn its pages that it's not only a book you read, it's also a book you do. Since 1989, I have developed spiritual health programmes that you can work through to enable you to come into a deeper walk with Jesus. These unique programmes will take you into the realm of meditation, memorising, Bible study, paraphrasing, writing a Psalm, etc. I am excited at the opportunities this book gives people to go deeper than they've ever gone before.

Another reason I have written these programmes is to help people who are struggling or who are counselling those who are struggling in their Christian walk. Several years ago, after counselling many individuals, I discovered that often people would look to me and not to God for the answer to their problem. Although I do believe that counsel from others is essential at times, it is important that people's dependence is on God rather than on a human source. Many times when people would come to me for help, I would spend time praying, fasting and seeking God for them while the counselee would relax because they were confident that I would hear from God. After a while, I began to feel that this wasn't quite how it should be! I started to ask them if they would be prepared to set aside time to pray, fast and seek God about their problem. I also began to think through how they should structure their time and that was how my programmes started.

The results I got from this were quite incredible. After spending some time fasting and praying and working their way through one of my programmes, they came back really excited that God had spoken to them for themselves. Some knew the answer to their problem and all I had to do was to thank God for what he had already done. With others, I discovered after reading their notes that my programmes saved me hours of counselling as it gave me a detailed account of their inner thoughts and helped me pray for them with greater understanding. However, this book is not only for those who have problems in their Christian life, it's for anyone who has a hunger in their heart to learn more of God and his word and be spiritually fit.

I have had many letters since the publication of my first three books on this subject telling me how much God has used the programmes to bring them into his deep and wonderful presence and experience a new freedom in Christ. Here's an extract from a letter, which really blessed me.

"I wanted to let you know that your book has ministered to me so much. I am a nineteen-year-old teenager and have spent all my teenage years in a children's home. After leaving the children's home, I found myself homeless, so for a while I lived on the streets and got involved in drugs. Throughout my life, I have been abused physically, emotionally and sexually.

After meeting some Christians, I decided to live my life for God, but I had one problem - God was not a reality to me. The church I attended was full of so much hurt and pain that instead of realising the people were not strong Christians and they were only human, I blamed God. I told him, 'If that's what Christianity is about, then I don't want it.' So much came against me that I went further and further away from God. I saw your book in a magazine and felt strongly that I should buy it, which I did. I read it and did your programmes and since that day, I am glad to say your book has changed my life. Instead of looking at people, I am looking at the one and only Almighty God and I'm learning to trust Him. I have now got the chance of working with the homeless people on the streets and know Jesus wants to affect their lives. I praise God for you, Nancy, for the help I and many others have received from your programmes."

A.J. - Scotland

Here's another from a man in Northern Ireland:

"At a time of deep depression and stress, I bought your book and decided to take a day off work and spend time doing one of your programmes. I could see myself going through life as a person of no consequence and no worth. I have scars from my childhood because my mother physically abused me. By doing your programme and fixing my eyes on Jesus, everything started to come into perspective. I have *been really challenged about dying to self. The trouble is that circumstances often overtake me and the old feelings of rejection return. I am learning that dying to self has to happen every day, every minute, through the good times as well as the bad. As I meditate on his goodness, I realise I am really in love with Jesus."*

T.M.

Here's another from someone who found my programmes helpful in discovering more of God:

"I have been meaning to write to you for a long time, but haven't managed it until now. I came across your book and as I looked at it, I thought I should take it home to have a closer look. God was just beginning at that point to do some major 'surgery' work in my personal life and clearly said that he wanted to use your book to transform my life. At the same time, he challenged me to fast two days a week for the entire three months that it would take to work through your book. Well, by early December, I had done all the programmes and I had completed a three-month partial fast. I can honestly say that never before in my Christian life has God done so much in me than in these past three months. Your book was thoroughly used by the Lord to challenge, shape, form and build me and I feel like I have gone through a tough training school that has changed a lot of my attitudes and matured my faith and walk with God.

I want to thank you.......this book was definitely in God's will for you to write because I'm sure he has not just used it in my life but will in countless others too."

T.S. - London

Here's a letter from a lady who continually finds the programmes very encouraging and helpful no matter how many times she does them.

"Over the years I have used your books, Spiritual Health Plan and Developing Spiritual Wholeness to tighten my intimacy with God and to see what he wants to show me using a structured workout. I was surprised recently when God spoke to me through one of your programmes about my forthcoming trip to Australia. I felt God say I should 'go in friendship' into a potentially difficult situation with relatives and acquaintances with whom there had been little contact in the past. What should I find but open arms of friendship and welcome everywhere I went with God building friendship, warmth and trust between us. I am so glad I had the simplicity of the message 'Go in friendship' and that brought such a depth and quality of friendship that I know will have a lasting effect. I also used your programme 'Growing in Intercession' to pray for Australia before my visit. God planted such a missionary zeal in me to pray for the people of that country - so much so that when we sang in church a song entitled, 'The Great Southland' I sang it with love and a sense of belonging that brought tears to my eyes.

Nancy, God has impacted me so many times over the years through your books and every time I think, 'Can there be more?' every time the answer is 'YES'."

J.R. - Bristol

I trust these letters encourage you to use these programmes and discover for yourself how much God is longing to take you deeper into his presence.

USING THE PROGRAMMES

In this book, I have written weekly programmes which give you 'bite sized' portions to work through each day, and then at the end of the book I have given you daily programmes which give you a plan to work through from 9am - 5pm. The latter programmes are very good if you are planning to set aside a day or a portion of a day to seek God.

I have written each weekly programme on a particular theme with an introductory passage to envision you into the plan. Each programme will run for seven days and gives thirty minutes of exercises for each day. You will notice that I have timed each exercise; however, the programme is designed to be flexible. Don't worry if your timing is different to what I have put down. The timings are only a guide for you. You will also notice that at the end of each chapter, I give a verse or thought for you to 'carry' with you throughout the week.

I have also recorded several meditation CDs which gives people music and meditations that will help them be released into the presence of God. I have included some of the mediations into the programmes therefore it will be helpful to you to use the CDs with this book. You can purchase these online at **www.nancygoudie.com** or on **www.ngm.org.uk/shop** or by calling 01454 414880.

Physical exercise is something that I don't find easy and yet when I've actually done it, I feel so much more relaxed and alert. Exercise is extremely good for you as it helps to release the tensions and stresses of everyday life. A number of years ago I was told by my doctor that I would have to be on high blood pressure pills for the rest of my life. I started taking the pills, but at the same time decided that I would exercise physically by swimming three times a week. Within time, I was taken off my blood pressure pills because my blood pressure was consistently normal without using the medication. Physical exercise is very good for you. Similarly, spiritual exercise is good for your spiritual life and should be undertaken regularly to keep you 'fit and healthy'. It always amazes me when I read about people who will spend hours exercising and training because they are dedicated to a particular sport. They are incredibly disciplined and will willingly sacrifice hours of their time. It is even more vital to be disciplined in our Christian life. However, it is important to note that while discipline by itself will not change us, it does put us in a place where God can change us. We don't want to get into legalism, but neither do we want to get lethargic in our walk with God. It is essential to be intimate with God and especially to have a vibrant daily friendship, which keeps us aware and responsive to what he's doing today.

Once you have completed a programme, do feel free to write to me and let me know what God has said and done with you. It is so encouraging for me to receive letters telling me how God had used the programmes to bring many into a deeper walk with Him. Send letters to Nancy Goudie, ngm, Caedmon Complex, Bristol Road, Thornbury, Bristol, BS35 3JA, UK or e-mail me at **nancy@nancygoudie.com**. I'd love to hear from you.

2 The Exercises

MEDITATION

One of the lost arts in the Christian world is meditation. However, whenever I mention the word meditation often people get concerned that we are getting into something dodgy! It sounds dodgy because often we associate it with Transcendental Meditation, Eastern Mysticism or the New Age Movement but actually the art of meditation has actually been stolen from us. Christian meditation is a wonderful refreshing way of hearing God speak and has been used since the beginning of time.

The Bible has many references to meditation. Let me give you a few scriptures that you can look up for yourself to discover that meditation is completely Biblical. **Joshua 1:8**; **Psalm 48:9**; **Genesis 24:63**; **Psalm 119:148** all tell us about meditation. Transcendental Meditation and the New Age movement tell us to empty our minds. This, I believe, can be very dangerous and I would never encourage anyone to do that. It allows outside influences, which are not always good, to invade our minds and affect our lives. In contrast, Christian meditation is allowing God and scripture to fill our minds. Quite a difference! It demands discipline since our minds find it easy to wander from one subject to another, however, if you are willing to try meditation, I know you will find it a very useful and fulfilling exercise. I have also discovered that for many people it is one of the easiest ways of hearing God speak to you. If you have never heard God speak to you - then do try meditation.

It was back in 1981 when I first heard about meditation. I was at a British Youth for Christ conference when Alex Buchanan, a wonderful man of God, asked us to meditate on a verse from scripture and then informed us that afterwards he would pick a couple of volunteers to share what they had received from God. I don't know about you, but when preachers say they will pick a few volunteers, I start to get nervous! In this case, I was even more so, because I hadn't a clue how to meditate.

I looked around me to see if there was anyone else as ignorant as me but everyone seemed to be looking intelligently at their Bibles. I thought, 'Great! Everyone here knows how to mediate and I know what's going to happen - he's going to pick me!' I sank really low in my chair, hoping Alex wouldn't see me and tried to pretend that I knew what to do. There was silence for a few minutes, then our friend Eric Delve, the National Evangelist for BYFC at the time, stood up and said, *"Alex, I'm sure I'm speaking on behalf of lots of people here, but I really don't know what to do. Would you teach us how to meditate?"* As relief flooded through my body, I praised God for his courage and honesty! It turned out that no one knew how to meditate; they only knew how to look as though they did. We were then shown how to meditate and since that time I have used meditation on numerous occasions in my own time with God, as well as teaching the practice to many others. It's a wonderful way of learning what God wants to teach us through his word.

So ... how do you meditate? Let me give you step-by-step instructions as to how to meditate on the Bible.

HOW TO MEDITATE

First of all, relax – it's very easy; so don't get uptight or anxious about it. If you do, then you will find it difficult to hear anything from God. Follow these simple instructions:

1. Look up the suggested scripture.
2. Read it slowly.
3. Pray and ask God to speak to you through it.
4. Read it again several times.
5. Spend time thinking about what the verse says.
6. Perhaps dwell on a phrase or section of the verse, or even just one word.
7. Allow yourself to follow a train of thought, until you see something in the verse you have never seen before.
8. Write down what you get.
9. If your mind begins to wander totally off the subject, then start again

Let me give you an example. I meditated on **John 15:4** which says, *'Remain in me, and I will remain in you. No branch can bear fruit by itself; it must remain in the vine. Neither can you bear fruit unless you remain in me.'*

Once I had read the verse through several times and asked God to speak to me, my attention was taken up with the last sentence. 'Neither can you bear fruit unless you remain in me'. One of my main aims in life is to produce 'fruit' in my life. I want God to use me to bring many into his Kingdom and to affect Christians' lives by bringing them closer to Him. At the same time, I want God to affect my life in such a way that the Holy Spirit and the 'fruit of the Spirit' is shown more and more so that there is less of me and more of him. God reminded me again when I meditated on this scripture that there is nothing I can do to bring these desires to pass, other than keeping close to him. If I remove myself from the vine, or in other words do not have a vibrant and living relationship with Jesus, then I cannot produce the kind of fruit that I would like to see happen. However, if my main priority in life is to love, serve and keep close to Jesus, then all the desires of my heart will be fulfilled. He reminded me of the verse in **Psalm 37:4** which was given to both Ray and me when we were called into full-time Christian work, which says, *'Delight yourself in the Lord and he will give you the desires of your heart.'* I finished my meditation by telling the Lord again that I want to be a close friend to him. I want to be someone whom he can trust with his plans and purposes. I committed myself to a deeper walk with him.

Although my meditation did not give any fresh insights into scripture this time, it focused my attention again upon the Lord and my relationship with him, and it reminded me of how important it was to 'remain in Him' and stirred up more of a desire to press on and go deeper with him. I know that as you try this kind of meditation, God will use it to strengthen and excite you on your spiritual journey.

USING YOUR IMAGINATION

Another type of meditation is using scripture, your imagination and perhaps music to bring you deeper into the presence of God. I have often used this form of meditation either by myself or with a large audience. The results coming from this form of meditation have been very exciting. At the end of the meditation, people have often been in tears, having heard from God or having been touched by God in a special way. I would encourage you to use this type of exercise and not to be fearful of using your imagination. When Jesus was here on earth he used to stimulate people's imaginations by telling stories that painted pictures in their minds. God created you with an imagination; therefore he does want you to use it to his glory, rather than in self-centred and unreal fantasising.

As I mentioned earlier, I have several CDs that work as companions to this book and are available from ngm. Each CD gives music and several spoken meditations so that you can get the full impact of having the music and the spoken meditation rather than trying to do the meditation from the written word only. I've outlined below a meditation that I have used personally which will help you get started.

HOW TO USE YOUR IMAGINATION IN MEDITATION

Play some music that does not have any lyrics on it (if you have purchased one of my meditation CDs then some of them have several tracks with music only on them. These would be ideal to use). Open your Bible at **Mark 15** and read from verse **21** to the end of chapter **16**. Then read **Luke 24:44** to **49**. Now I want you to read the following meditation and use your imagination to be part of the story. Imagine yourself to be one of the people who followed Jesus during his ministry here on earth.

Crucified

The last few years with Jesus have just been tremendous. You have come to love and believe in him. You have seen him do incredible miracles in front of your eyes and the wisdom coming from him is amazing. He seems to know the right thing to say in each situation. He makes you feel important and deeply loved. No one has loved you the way Jesus has. He has become a special friend. Surely he must be the Messiah, the one you've been waiting for. However, this morning you have heard news that must be wrong. Someone came to your door and told you that Jesus was arrested last night and that the authorities were going to kill him today. Fear and panic rise in your being. Jesus has had death threats before - surely he will just walk away from this as he has done in the past?

You begin to calm down - Jesus will do something, surely! You decide to go and see for yourself. Out in the street, everyone is talking about Jesus being arrested. You overhear snippets of conversation about him being taken to Golgotha (the Place of the Skull where they often crucify people). You run outside the city and there you meet up with the others who cared and provided for Jesus and as you look Jesus is being laid on a cross. Everything within you screams 'NO!' as you hear the hammer knocking the nails into his hands and feet. There are many throwing insults at Jesus, mocking him and you want to stop them, but fear and bewilderment hold you back. 'What's going on Jesus? What's happening? What about all the plans we had for the future? You are the Messiah - come down from the cross, show them who you really are'. But Jesus stays there, hanging, dying.

Darkness covers the whole land. The sun disappears as though it does not want to shine on a day like today. The women around you are weeping, the disciples, Jesus' close friends are all confused. This cannot be happening. Suddenly, Jesus calls out, *'Father, into your hands, I commit my Spirit'*.

It's all over. He's dead! The friend you loved and trusted has gone. Confusion and fear are raging within you. You wait with the others until the body of Jesus is taken down from the cross. You follow them and see them placing the body into a tomb. Together with some women you decide to visit his tomb to anoint his body with spices after the Sabbath.

Very early on the first day of the week, you meet together and hurry towards the tomb. You talk about how you are going to remove the huge stone, which they have rolled across the entrance. However, when you reach the tomb, you notice that the stone has already been rolled away and the guards who are supposed to be watching the tomb have disappeared. 'What's happened? You walk into the tomb and see a young man sitting there in a white robe who tells you that Jesus is alive. JESUS IS ALIVE? What does he mean? How can he be? You are bewildered and you notice that your hands are trembling. You start to run to tell his disciples, but someone stands in front of you. You look up and there standing in front of you is *Jesus*. Joy and excitement suddenly fill your being as you exclaim, 'YOU'RE ALIVE, YOU'RE ALIVE!' You fall to the ground and worship him. Jesus - you're alive!

After your meditation, note down how you felt as you went through the story. Write down any lessons you have learned by being part of this story. Writing things down is always very helpful, not only at the time, as it gives you a way to assess your thoughts more clearly, but also at a later stage when you need encouragement from God. It is always good to look over your notes and see what God has said to you. Thank God for his plans and purposes for your life and tell him that you will trust him for the future, because you know he is faithful and all powerful and will bring into being those things he has promised. Spend time praising and worshipping him for who he is.

I'm sure as you use your imagination to bring you face to face with Jesus, you will find that the Lord will use this method of meditation to speak directly into your life and touch you in a new fresh way.

USING OBJECTS OR NATURE IN MEDITATION

I also encourage people to meditate on nature, a flower, a stone, a fruit or a tree perhaps and ask God to speak through it. The results have been incredible. I am always amazed at how much people can get through meditating on nature or on an object. At my weekend conferences, which I hold every year in a luxury hotel in Bristol and Preston, I often encourage people to meditate this way. One lady who meditated on a kiwi fruit said this, *"The first thing that struck me about the inside of the kiwi was that it seemed to have the shape of a sun with rays coming from it. I felt God saying that although we can feel a bit like the outside of the kiwi - perhaps a bit dull and boring - that actually the light of God is constantly burning inside us. God also pointed out to me that in between the rays were lots of little seeds. I sensed God was saying that he has planted seeds in me through the years which he is still nurturing and that one day they will blossom into beautiful things for God."*

I have also used chocolate in meditation. Although this is a fun way to meditate, God has often spoken to people so deeply through this. Basically God can speak through anything, it really doesn't matter what it is. In the Bible, God spoke through a donkey and if God can speak through a donkey then surely he can speak through chocolate. Try meditating on chocolate using the five senses that God has given you and you will be astonished at how easy it is to hear him speak to you.

It is important to realise that because the enemy often tries to deceive us, we should always make sure that what we receive from God through meditation is consistent with scripture. Share what you receive with your pastor, spiritual leader or someone whom you respect in God. I will speak more about this in The Prayer Workout.

Here are some more exercises to help draw you closer to God.

WRITING A PSALM

Whenever I mentioned to the people attending my conference or one of my spiritual exercise seminars that we are all going to write a psalm, a look of horror appears on a number of faces. Looks of *"You will never get me to do that"* and *"Well that's it, I may as well give up now"* are common. However, if people take the plunge and decide to go for it, then they discover writing a psalm to be a new and exciting way of putting their thoughts and feelings about God on paper. The first time we did this exercise in Heartbeat (a band that my husband and I founded in the '80's), I felt exactly the same. The fact that I was surrounded by people who wrote music did not add to my confidence! However, when I put pen to paper and I concentrated on my Heavenly Dad, a great explosion of praise happened within me and I just wrote down what I was feeling. It doesn't need to rhyme or have fancy or flowery words. It just needs to convey your love for God in a way that reflects your personality. Try reading one of the Psalms in the Bible before you start. **Psalm 100** is a great psalm of praise. Here's a psalm of mine.

Lord, you are my dearest friend,
Someone in whom I can love and trust,
Someone who is faithful and will never let me down,
Someone who has stood with me throughout the passage of time.
How I love you so!

Your arms of love surround me and I feel safe and secure,
There's nowhere I would rather be, than living close to you.
No one else can match your love - nothing else comes close,

I would rather have you than all the tea in China,
How I love you so!

Even when times are tough and I do not understand
All that I am going through. It just does not make sense.
You come with your gentle answer - 'Just trust me anyway.'
Lord, where else can I turn? You alone have all the answers.
How I love you so!

PARAPHRASING

Here is another exercise that people shy away from and yet when they experience it they realise how much it can help you get to grips with the Bible. Sometimes we pass over the more difficult parts of the Bible and if someone asked us to explain what we have read, we wouldn't know how to go about it. Paraphrasing can really help you understand the meaning behind the words. Paraphrasing is a fancy word for using your own words to express the meaning of the passage. We need to be careful that we don't change the meaning of the passage but just express it in a different manner. After you have paraphrased a piece of scripture, look up The Message or The Living Bible, which are paraphrases of the Bible, or perhaps look up a commentary to see if you have altered the meaning at all. Try the following verse and you will see how easy it is.

Read **Romans 8:1** -'*Therefore, there is now no condemnation for those who are in Christ Jesus.'*

Here's what it says in the Living Bible: *'So there is now no condemnation awaiting those who belong to Christ Jesus.'*

Here's my paraphrase: *'Because of all that Jesus has done for us and because we know him as a friend, we do not need to live in guilt and shame.'*

Now try writing yours.

MEMORISING

When I was a child, I was taught by my parents to memorise scripture. Memorising the Bible was fairly common then, but over the years this is a practice that seems to have diminished. There are many reasons why it is important to have scripture stored in our minds. Here are a few to encourage you.

1. God has told us to do so. **Deuteronomy 11:18**.
2. It helps in moments of weakness or temptation; e.g. when the enemy tempts Jesus, he fights back by quoting scripture. **Matthew 4:4**.
3. It is really helpful when we are sharing our faith with others. **Hebrews 4:12** says that God's word is sharper than a two-edged sword.
4. It is helpful in finding God's direction and guidance for our lives. **Proverbs 3:1-6**.

The main excuse for not memorising scripture is that your memory is bad. However, I love to inform people that your memory can be trained to retain information. It's usually because of lack of use that your memory isn't working as well as it used to.

The best way to memorise is to break the verse into portions. Learn the first portion first, then the first and the second together, then the first, second and third together and so on until you have completed the task.

Let's take **1 Thessalonians 5:16-18** as an example. It reads like this:

Be joyful always; pray continually; give thanks in all circumstances, for this is God's will for you in Christ Jesus.

These verses naturally fall into phrases. So, let's take the first phrase, *'Be joyful always.'* Repeat that out loud many times, then add the second phrase: *'Be joyful always; pray continually.'* Again repeat it a number of times before adding the third phrase: *'Be joyful always; pray continually; give thanks in all circumstances.* Repeat the same process before adding the fourth phrase; *'Be joyful always; pray continually; give thanks in all circumstances for this is God's will for you in Christ Jesus.'*

Once you have said it all, say it over and over again until it becomes part of you. It helps to get it firmly implanted in the brain. Perhaps put it on a card or piece of paper and take it with you in order that you can review it during the day. It is worth noting, however, that just because you can say something once or twice doesn't necessary mean you have memorised it. It needs reviewing in order for it to be imprinted in your memory banks.

In these days when there is so much garbage thrown at us from our society through the media, etc., it's so important to fill our minds with God's word. In **Philippians 4:8** Paul tells us to fill our minds with whatever is true, noble, right, pure, lovely, excellent and praiseworthy, because, as you are probably aware, whatever you fill your mind with eventually begins to affect your lifestyle. That's one of the reasons why it is so important to memorise scripture.

FASTING

Most people feel the task of fasting is beyond them. How could they possibly do without food for a specific period of time? I thought that myself when I first heard about fasting. However, I have found over the years that prayer and fasting together make a very powerful combination. If you've never fasted before, let me encourage you, you will not die through fasting for a few days.

Everyone who joins ngm (new generation music) learns how to fast unless they cannot because of medical reasons. A few years ago we discovered that one of our new teams had decided that in order to celebrate getting through their first day without food, they would have a bean feast at midnight. We announced to the teams that when we fast for a day it means consuming no food until the following morning; therefore all 'bean feasts' were out. One girl approached Ray afterwards really upset and told him she would not sleep, and in fact would not survive the night, if she didn't eat something before going to bed. Ray assured her that she wouldn't die and in fact she came back the next day and apologised. She is not alone in thinking that if you fast more than one meal you will die. There are many people who think fasting is harmful for you. The truth is, that rather than being bad for you, fasting is extremely good for your body. When you fast, the energy that is normally used to digest, etc., is then spent in purifying the body. Fasting cleanses the blood stream, which results in better health. It certainly makes you aware of how much we seem to be ruled in our lives by our stomachs.

Although there are many physical benefits from fasting, don't fast just because you need to lose weight. If you need to diet, then there are many good diets around which can help you lose weight in a sensible and controlled manner. Your reasons for fasting should be much deeper than the desire to lose weight.

REASONS FOR FASTING

Apart from the many reasons why it is good for our physical bodies to fast, there are also many spiritual reasons why we should fast, the main one being that Jesus expects us to fast. You only have to read your Bible to discover this to be the case. Read **Matthew 9:15** and also **Matthew 6:16**. Fasting should not be an optional extra. When we combine prayer with fasting, God's power is released into the situations for which we are praying.

There are many people in the Bible who fasted for various reasons. Let me give you a few people and their reasons for fasting.

1. *Jesus* **Matthew 4:2**; Jesus fasted before his earthly ministry started.
2. *Daniel* **Daniel 10**; Daniel fasted to receive more revelation from God.
3. *David* **2 Samuel 12:16**; David fasted to plead with God to change his mind.
4. *Esther* **Esther 4:16**; Esther fasted before warfare.
5. *Jehoshaphat* **2 Chronicles 20:3**; he and the whole of Judah fasted for deliverance.
6. *The leaders of the church at Antioch* **Acts 13:2**; they fasted to discern more of God's will.

You may have other reasons why you should want to fast but I do hope these few inspire you.

I believe fasting holds your prayer request constantly before God even though there may be times in your busy schedule when it is difficult for you to talk to God. Also, if you are finding that you just cannot break through in one or more areas of your life, then do add fasting to your prayers. I fast regularly for many different reasons, but my main reason is that I want God to anoint me more and more for what he has called me to be and do. I have to say that since I began to fast regularly some years ago, my life has completely been changed. It is a discipline that I would recommend to anyone, but particularly to those who want to go deeper with God.

No one finds fasting easy, because everything within you fights against it. However, the good news is that it does get easier the more you do it.

WHAT IS FASTING?

Fasting primarily means consuming no food, and perhaps even no water, for spiritual reasons, over a period of time.

There are three main ways of fasting:

a. **Partial fast** Eating simple basic food, or liquids only.
b. **Normal fast** No food, water only or drinks e.g., fruit juices, etc. (Do not go beyond forty days - see below.)
c. **Absolute fast** No food or water. (Do not go beyond three days - see below.)

There are other ways of fasting that do not include food:

a. **A sleep fast** Spending a half or whole night in prayer. Or even getting up a few hours earlier than normal to spend quality time with God.

b. **A television fast** Deciding not to watch television for a period of time. We have often used this type of fasting when it was impossible to fast food. I'm sure if you use this type of fasting you will find it not only refreshing but also very revealing. I guess we all spend too much time sitting in front of the box.

c. **A favourite fast** If there is a particular food or drink that you really like, then why not fast it for some time? God once told a good friend of ours to stop eating his favourite snack of Coke and crisps for a while. Ray also spends time fasting his favourite drink now and then.

You can fast and pray as an individual (**Psalm 35:13**), as a family (**1 Samuel 31:13**), as a church (**Acts 13:1-3**) or even as a nation (**Leviticus 16:29**). Some time ago, our church fasted corporately for three days to seek more of God. We decided that we would ask our son, Daniel who was seven at the time, if he would join us. He had seen us fasting many times so he knew it meant giving up something, usually food. We asked him what he would like to give up and he decided he would like to give up sweets for the three days. It was really great to be able to fast together as a family and as a church.

HOW TO FAST

Let me give you some fasting tips:

1. Do start slowly - especially if you've never fasted before. Try cutting out one meal then increase your fasting as time goes on. Don't promise the Lord that you will fast many days if in fact you have never fasted even a meal before. Start slowly and build up.
2. If you are a young person who is still living at home with your parents, then do speak with them about your desire to fast. If your parents are not Christians and forbid you to fast, then do remember there are other ways of fasting besides going without food. Also, if you share a house with someone, then do let them know you are fasting. Not only will it let them know to be sensitive, but it will also let them know not to cook you a meal. Do remember though, not to brag about your fasting to others (see **Matthew 6:16-18**).
3. If you experience headaches during the fast, this may be due to caffeine withdrawal. It is wise to cut down on coffee, tea, coke and even chocolate beforehand as they all contain caffeine. It's always easier to fast *without* a headache!
4. To combat hunger pangs: fool your stomach by drinking lots of water or liquid.
5. Don't be put off by the fact that you are working. You can easily fast whilst working unless your job is a heavy manual one. We would never advise our teams to fast when they are on mission and have to move lots of heavy equipment. Be wise, but don't make your work your excuse.
6. Try brushing your teeth many times during the day to keep your breath fresh. If this is impossible, then use

mints or breath freshener sprays.

7. If you forget you are fasting and eat something, don't lose heart. God will not stop listening to you. I remember one day when I was fasting, I ate a strawberry which we had grown in our garden. It was in my mouth half eaten when I suddenly remembered that I was still fasting. Don't give up at that point, just apologise to the Lord and keep on going.

8. Break your fast *slowly*, perhaps with fruit or a light salad.

9. Do not fast food and water for more than three days as the body cannot cope without water beyond that time.

10. Do not fast food for more than forty days as the body cannot cope beyond this time. You would need God's divine help to fast for more than forty days. If you fast for more than three days, then I would recommend getting support, help and wisdom from your spiritual leaders.

A word of warning! If you are on medication for a serious illness such as heart problems, diabetes, liver or kidney disease, then I would strongly recommend that you **do not fast without consulting your doctor**.

HOW LONG SHOULD I FAST?

Personally, I would recommend fasting regularly. Perhaps do a twenty-four or thirty-six-hour fast once a week with a longer fast as and when the Lord leads you. I have found regular fasting to be incredibly uplifting in my spiritual life as well as beneficial in my physical body. I want God to continue to help me and mould me to be more like Jesus and I've discovered that fasting is one way of giving God an opportunity of doing something deeper in me.

If you have never fasted before, then as I said above, don't decide to start with a forty-day normal fast! Try missing one meal first, then progress to two meals. Then try a twenty-four-hour fast, i.e., stopping eating after 7pm one night and then miss all meals the next day and start eating again at 7pm. Perhaps you could then try a thirty-six-hour fast, which would mean stop eating at 7pm one night, then missing all meals the next day and breaking your fast the following morning with breakfast. It is possible to fast up to forty days, but this is an exceptionally long time and should only be undertaken if you are absolutely sure that God has told you to do so. I would recommend that you should only take on a longer fast, and by that I mean more than three days, if you get clear guidance from God and have submitted your plans to your spiritual leaders, in order that they can help, encourage and give you wisdom throughout your fast.

I would also *strongly* recommend that you only embark on an absolute fast if you receive direct instructions from God and if your church leadership witness your call from God to do so. Do remember that an absolute fast should not go beyond three days as the body cannot cope without water beyond that time. On both the forty-day normal fast and the three-day absolute fast, we would need God's divine help in order to survive beyond these timings.

It's important to know that fasting is not intended to be a crude attempt to express our spirituality, but it is one way of coming closer to God. Please don't feel condemned by thinking that a forty-day fast is for 'spiritual giants' and that you can only manage twenty-four hours! The important thing is to be obedient to God and not simply to undertake a marathon when he may only want us to attempt a gentle jog.

HOW TO BREAK A FAST

It is important that you break your fast *slowly*. I would recommend fruit, vegetables or a light salad. Do not break a fast with food that is heavy and greasy. I know from experience that this is a very silly thing to do and upsets your system, sometimes quite badly. I know one guy who broke a reasonably long fast with a hot and spicy Indian meal and ended up in hospital. Do remember that the longer the fast, the more gradually you should break it. Although your stomach will have shrunk during your fast, your eyes are just as big, and the temptation is that you allow your eyes to judge how much you should eat and not your stomach. Exercise your self-control and ask God to help you come off the fast sensibly.

HOW TO GET MAXIMUM BENEFIT FROM A FAST

Spiritual and physical preparation for fasting will help you get the maximum benefit from it. If you are going on a fast that is longer than twenty-four hours, then it is important to cut down on your food intake the day before. I would suggest going on a fruit or vegetable diet during the previous day. If you are used to drinking ordinary tea and coffee, then you may experience headaches during your fast. As I already advised you in the fasting tips, in order to avoid this cut out tea and coffee a few days beforehand. A headache during your fast can greatly hinder what you would like to accomplish.

As well as preparing physically, it is very important to prepare spiritually. Before embarking on your fast, write down what you want God to accomplish in you or through you during your time of self-denial. Decide how you are going to spend your day. How much time are you going to be able to put aside for prayer, study, etc? Decide how to structure your day and decide that nothing will get in the way. For some of you who have put a day or two aside to reach out to God through prayer and fasting - you may want to use the longer day programmes at the end of the book. You will notice that I have given programmes that will be ideal to use on this kind of retreat with God. Pray and ask God for his protection on you, your family and your possessions. On a practical note make sure you have bought enough drinks for your fast day.

I've often noticed that when some people fast, they will have the attitude of "How much can I get away with here?" The question should not be "How little can I give up for God?" but rather "How much can I give up for God?" King David said in **2 Samuel 24:24**, *"I will not sacrifice to the Lord my God burnt offerings that cost me nothing."* Let's fast with a generous heart towards God, with joy and delight at serving our God. He's so worth it - isn't he? Fasting is not something that should be dreaded or seen as a punishment, it should be seen as a privilege. If we can see situations change in the unseen realm because of our fasting - isn't that a real privilege?

PRAYER

I heard someone say recently, *"Prayer is the most talked about subject in the Church of God and is also the least practised in the Church of God."* How true! Prayer is something that we all know we should do, but sometimes find very difficult. I don't think I have ever encountered anyone who has said that they find prayer to be easy. Perhaps you think that you are the only person who struggles in this area, but that's not true. We all struggle with prayer at times. It seems that every time we start to pray, the phone will ring, or the doorbell will go, or we think of a hundred and one different things we should have done. I'm sure this happens because the enemy knows how effective our prayers are and will try at any cost to keep us from communicating with Heaven. Satan knows that if he keeps us from praying then he has defeated us. It's important to recognise that our prayers do accomplish much and that communication between our Heavenly Father and ourselves is essential.

As well as finding time to have special intimate times with God, I also try to keep my communication open with Him twenty-four hours a day. I talk to him no matter where I am and no matter what I'm doing, even if it's a very small thing like trying to find a parking space. God is interested in the small problems we have in life as well as the big ones.

FREEDOM IN PRAYER

We should never restrict our friendship with God to ten minutes in the morning and the same in the evening. If we do, then what happens is that when you miss your 'quiet time', you feel guilty for the rest of the day and often think that nothing will go right for that day. God doesn't just want a little slot in your day – he wants you! He wants a constant open friendship with you throughout the day. It is important to set aside quality time for God, but when that is impossible one day, if you have a constant friendship with him, then your relationship doesn't have to be 'put on hold' until the next time you can give him quality time. You can speak to him no matter where you are, telling him what is going on in your life and asking for his help. When I first discovered this, a real freedom came into my walk with God. No longer was I locked into legalism but was free to have a relationship with him no matter where I was.

Prayer is something that we all need to learn. In **Luke 11:1**, the disciples asked Jesus to teach them to pray. These were people who knew what it was like to pray and had been taught from their earliest years that they should pray to God. Their whole nation prayed, so why did they ask Jesus *how* to pray? There must have been something different about Jesus' prayers. I believe that if we look at Jesus' prayers in the Bible we will discover that he prayed with authority and boldness that emphasised His intimate relationship with his Heavenly Father. When Jesus prayed, things happened. No wonder his way of praying was so desirable. I feel in my own life I have still so much to learn about prayer. I often echo the request of the disciples, *"Lord, teach me how to pray."* Let's learn to pray the way Jesus did. I've listed below a few things we can learn from the way he prayed.

1. He prayed out loud

I'm always amazed at how many hands go up when I ask people in seminars to indicate if they 'think' their prayers rather than 'speak' their prayers. There is nothing wrong in 'thinking' your prayers; however, if you do, then it can lead to wandering thoughts, whereas 'talking' your prayers helps you to focus so much better. I would encourage you to talk your prayers as much as you can. Not only will it help you in your own time with God, but it will also help you when it comes to praying publicly. There are many of Jesus' prayers recorded for us in the Bible, therefore he must have prayed out loud, e.g., **John 17, John 11:41**. Even on the cross Jesus 'spoke' his prayer of forgiveness (**Luke 23:34**). There is also something very powerful in actually speaking out what you believe to be true. There is power in the spoken word.

2. He was intimate

He spoke to God as if he really knew him and even called him his 'Daddy'. Jesus had an intimate friendship with his Heavenly Dad, which had developed from before time began. God wants to get to know us intimately and the only way to do that is to talk with him often. If you wanted to develop a friendship with someone, the way you would do that is to communicate with them. If you tried to talk with someone but they ignored you, then eventually you would give up and walk away. Friendship means you need to have communication in both directions.

3. He prayed anywhere

Jesus prayed at a funeral (**John 11:41**); in a garden (**Mark 14:32**); on a mountain (**Matthew 14:23**); in lonely places (**Mark 1:35**); on a cross (**Mark 15:34**). In other words, he prayed no matter where he was. Throughout my programmes I have suggested that you go out for a walk with God. I have often found walking and talking with God to be a good way to pray and I would encourage you to try it. I recognise that the environments around you will be vastly different depending on where you live; those in the city will see things differently to those who are in the country. However, I would encourage you no matter where you live to speak to God when you walk with him and hear God speak to you through what you see around you. In my programmes I have often limited your walk to ten minutes because of time, but of course you can extend that time if you wish. Some people may so enjoy walking and talking with God that they spend hours with him in this way.

4. He was specific
Jesus did not pray in generalities but was specific (**Luke 23:34**). So often when we come to God in prayer, we pray around the issue rather than telling God exactly what we need him to do.

5. He was persistent
If you look at **Mark 8:22-25** where it tells the story of Jesus praying for the healing of a blind man at Bethsaida, you will see that Jesus was persistent in his prayers. Jesus quite clearly taught us in **Luke 11:5-10** and **Luke 18:1-8** that we should pray and not give up.

6. He prayed in faith
Jesus taught his disciples to pray with faith. Read **Mark 11:22-24**. There is little point in praying for a specific thing to happen if we pray without any expectation that he will do what we ask. Let's ask God to increase our faith in him to trust him for more.

7. He prayed with others

Jesus taught his disciples how important it was to pray with others in **Matthew 18:19-20**. Many people, including myself, find it easier to pray with others than they do on their own. At times, Jesus asked his disciples to watch and pray with him (**Matthew 26:36-38** and **Luke 9:28**). One thing Ray and I discovered in our married life was how important it was to pray together. The old saying is true, 'Those who pray together, stay together.' Your relationship with your wife/husband is much stronger if you learn to pray with one another. **Ecclesiastes 4:12** tells us that 'A cord of three strands is not quickly broken'. When we bring God into the centre of our relationships they become so much stronger.

8. He submitted to his Father's will

In **Luke 22:42**, Jesus prays to his Father in the Garden of Gethsemane and says, *"Father, if you are willing, take this cup from me; yet not my will, but yours be done."* Jesus willingly submitted to the will of the Father and in fact states quite clearly in **John 4:34**, *"My food is to do the will of him who sent me and to finish his work."* There will be times in our prayer life where we will pray for something and God quite clearly says *"No"*. A friend of mine just recently told me of a time when she was pregnant and she and her husband had prayed and asked God to give her a natural birth. However, when it came to the time for the baby to be born, he was born by caesarean section. They were disappointed and couldn't understand why God hadn't answered their prayers. When their next child was about to be born, they again asked God if they could have a natural birth, but when the child was born it also was born by caesarean section. Again, disappointment filled them and they expressed this to a doctor who was a friend and also a Christian and who just happened to be at the birth. They couldn't believe his reply. He said, *"Well, actually, if God had answered your prayer, I reckon both your babies would have died at birth, because your pelvis is too small for a natural birth."* They then understood why God had chosen to say *"No"* to their prayers. It's good to know when we pray that although God may not answer our prayers the way we want, he knows what is best!

HOW TO HEAR FROM GOD

Another barrier to prayer is that people find it hard to hear God's voice. Sometimes, because of rejection or insecurity, people can miss the voice of God and therefore their growth in him is stunted. The first thing we need to know is that God loves each of us and *wants* to communicate with us. We do not serve a God who is dead nor a God who is dumb. He loves each of us so deeply and enjoys an intimate relationship with us.

I am no more special in God's Kingdom than you are - God loves us all and therefore if I can hear from Heaven then so can you. That's not to say that I always find it easy to hear from God. There are times when it can be a real struggle and sometimes it can feel as though he is just not around. It's in those times that it's important to cling on to God and persist in prayer. In **Luke 18:1-8** Jesus stresses the importance of persisting in prayer.

A long time ago, I went through a number of weeks/ months where I found it very difficult to hear from God or even to feel his presence around me. I had often heard of people talking of 'the dark night of the soul' and had never quite understood what they meant. I wondered whether

God was displeased with me because I had done something to offend him, so I examined myself and asked God to highlight anything wrong in me. I repented of anything and everything I could think of, but still I could not hear from Heaven or feel God around me. Eventually, I cried out to God and told him that even if I didn't feel his presence or hear his voice, I would still hold on to Him. I felt like Peter in **John 6:68** who said to Jesus, *"Lord, to whom shall we go? You have the words of eternal life."* Where else could I go? I decided, even if I didn't feel him around me or couldn't hear his voice, to believe what the Bible tells me in **Hebrews 13:5**, that God will never leave me nor forsake me. In **Matthew 28:20** Jesus also says, *"And surely I will be with you always, to the very end of the age."* Throughout many months of tears and disappointment, I could only cling on to God's word.

There were times when I got annoyed with God because I couldn't understand what he was doing. I often had to ask him for his forgiveness and tell him that even though I didn't understand why I couldn't hear from him, I would trust him anyway. I think I cried more through those months than I had in all my previous years. It felt like 'a dark night of the soul'. It was in those dark days when I came to appreciate more fully friends who prayed for me and encouraged me with words that they had heard from the Lord. After a number of months, without explanation, God's presence suddenly returned and once more I found it a real joy to listen and hear from God.

Listening to God is an important part of prayer and therefore it is important to learn how to tune in to him. There are many ways that God uses to speak to us - The Bible; visions or pictures; dreams; people; sermons;

prophetic words; an audible voice; a still small voice, etc.

The main thing is to let God know that you are keen to hear from him and ask him to teach you how to listen. I have found that many people who have said they cannot hear God speak to them, actually have heard him speak but they have not recognised his voice. When we first learn to hear from God, it is a bit like 'tuning in' to a radio station. It takes time and effort to get by all the different sounds and signals you hear before you eventually find the exact programme you want. Sometimes, you feel like giving up, but when you persevere it is always worth it in the end. Listening to God can be just like that. Keep 'tuning in' to him and don't give up, because in the end it will be worth it. If you feel you have never heard from God, then one of the easiest ways of hearing God speak to you is through meditation on scripture. Why not try it and see?

CHECK OUT WHAT YOU HAVE HEARD

It is of *utmost importance* that we test everything we believe we have heard from God with his written word. God will *never* contradict what he has already said in the Bible. Do remember that although the enemy at all times wants to deceive us, we can protect ourselves by submitting our 'words from God' to our spiritual leaders. We are encouraged in **1 Thessalonians 5:21** to 'Test everything. Hold on to the good.'

STUDYING THE BIBLE

When I was younger, Bible study seemed to me to be only for vicars or ministers with theology degrees and not for someone like me, however, when I started to study the Bible for myself, I was amazed at how much I enjoyed it. As a young girl from Eastbourne discovered, Bible study can be exciting. She wrote to me and said

"I spent today doing one of your programmes and I have never before got so much from studying God's word. Thank you for giving me a structure that brings the scriptures alive."
J.F.

If you have never studied the Bible before, can I encourage you to try it? The Bible is the most amazing book with many diamonds, pearls and jewels just beneath the surface waiting to be found. I know you will find it exciting and encouraging. In my programmes, I have given you certain passages of scripture to study but have made it easier for you by asking questions. I have been really blessed preparing them, so my prayer is that you will be equally blessed doing them. Do write and let me know how you have got on.

You will also find that at times I have prepared self-help questions. These questions will help you to think through issues for yourself and also help you analyse why you feel or act the way you do. I hope you not only discover more about yourself through them, but that you also discover more about God and his ways.

You also may be interested to know that I have Bible Reading planners, which take you through the Bible in a year or two years. I started using a Bible planner to systematically read through the Bible in 1979 and have found it a fantastic way of reading the whole Bible every year. It is so important that we get to know the Bible for ourselves. Often people will just open the Bible and wonder what passage to read. They discard Leviticus and Ecclesiastes as too much like hard work and finally decide to read their favourite portion of the Bible once again! Using a Bible planner means that you know each day where to read and before long you have read your way from cover to cover. I recommend that everyone tries a Bible planner as I am sure you will find that your walk with God greatly increases in intimacy and knowledge - mine certainly did! You can purchase a Bible Reading Planner online at **www.ngm.org.uk/shop** or at **www.nancygoudie.com** or you can call the ngm office on 01454 414880.

PRAISE AND WORSHIP

Worship is not just something we do on Sundays in our church meetings; it is a *way of life*. The most important thing is not where we worship, but that we live in an attitude of worship before the Lord. It's interesting to note that **1 Kings 1:47** tells us that King David worshipped on his bed!

WORSHIP AS A LIFESTYLE

Romans 12:1 tells us to offer our *'bodies as living sacrifices, holy and pleasing to God'* as this is our spiritual act of worship. In **Genesis 22** we read that Abraham and Isaac went to a mountain to worship the Lord. Abraham went knowing that God had told him to sacrifice his son as a burnt offering. He came to worship God and lay down someone in his life who was extra special to him. He wasn't just coming to 'sing songs'; he was coming to sacrifice. He was giving God everything and nothing was being kept back. What an example to us when we come to worship God.

My desire is that I live my life in such a way that my whole life is worship to God, and that when I do speak or sing out my praise and worship of my King, I will hold nothing back. Can I encourage you to find new depths in your praise and worship of God?

In some of my programmes, I have included time for you to praise and worship the Lord. Whatever is happening in your life, no matter what problems you are encountering, come into his presence and worship him. My husband has written many worship songs; his latest songs are on a new ngm worship CD called 'Assured'. You can purchase this on **www.ngm.org.uk/shop**.

A number of years ago two good friends of mine Neil and Zoe Edbrooke went through an extremely tough time. Zoe at the time was the main worship leader at a church in Bristol. Neil had been very ill for some time and his health had been a great concern to all of us. Zoe not only looked after their four children, but also nursed Neil and helped him through the really bleak times. I saw her in tears many times as she has watched her husband suffer, yet she is a woman who was determined to praise God through the problems. When she led the worship at church, she gave her all. She may not have felt like praising, but she did it anyway with all her strength because she knew God was worth it. She was such an inspiration to those who watched her. Let's determine to praise God, despite our circumstances, because he is worthy at all times.

There are many ways of praising and worshipping God, which I will list for you. All of them are Biblical and I would encourage you to explore each way and add more of your own. Of course, I am sure you know that it's not the ways in themselves which are worship, but they are only an outward expression of the praise and worship we have in our hearts for God.

BIBLICAL WAYS TO EXPRESS PRAISE AND WORSHIP

1. Singing	**Colossians 3:16**
2. Singing in the Spirit	**1 Corinthians 14:15**
3. Singing out a new song	**Psalm 96:1**
4. Clapping hands	**Psalm 47:1**
5. Raising hands	**Psalm 134:2**;
	1 Timothy 2:8
6. Speaking	**Psalm 145:6-7**
7. Shouting	**Ezra 3:10-13**
8. Playing an instrument in worship	**Psalm 150:3-5**
9. Dancing	**Psalm 150:4; 2**
	Samuel 6:14-15
10. Leaping/jumping	**Acts 3:8**
11. Standing	**2 Chronicles 20:19**
12. Being still	**Psalm 46:10**
13. Bowing	**2 Chronicles 20:18**;
	Matthew 2:11;
	Nehemiah 8:6
14. Kneeling	**Psalm 95:6-7**
15. Lying prostrate	**Revelation 5:14**
	and **11:16**

Don't be afraid of trying new ways to praise and worship the Lord. If you have never sung out a 'new song' to the Lord before, then why not try it? If it makes your praise and worship times more real to you and more of a blessing to God, then that's what you want to achieve.

In **1 Kings 1:40**, when all the people were celebrating their new king, it says, *'And all the people went up after him, playing flutes and rejoicing greatly, so that the ground shook with the sound.'* I'm sure that their praise and worship must have been really noisy and creative. Let's make the ground shake with our praise and worship, after all, we have a King who is greater than Solomon. Let's give him the praise he so rightly deserves.

WHAT YOU WILL NEED FOR A PROGRAMME

Before you start working on a programme, let me list a few things you will need.

1. A Bible. (Most of the references I have given you are from the New International Version, so you might want to use that translation.)
2. A note pad and pen.
3. You may need a dictionary, depending on which programme you choose.
4. You may need a commentary of the Bible for some of the information needed in the Bible studies. If you don't own one, then you may be able to borrow one from a friend, or your church leader.
5. Once you have decided which programme you would like to do, look through it to see what items you need, e.g., it may help to play a worship CD to help you whilst you worship.
6. Making sure you have a room where you will not be disturbed is essential.
7. If you are fasting at any time during your programme, then do make sure you prepare yourself beforehand. Cut down on tea and coffee and perhaps go on a fruit or vegetable diet the day before.
8. Make sure you read the chapter on your particular theme before embarking on the programme. Perhaps read it the evening before you commence. This should help you be much more focused and envisioned.

9. Do remember that the timings are only a guide. Don't worry if you take longer or complete a particular exercise quicker.
10. Take time at the beginning of every day to ask the Holy Spirit to lead you to the secret place where you can be drenched in the presence of God.

My prayer for you as you work your way through this book is that your relationship with God will become stronger and stronger. I pray as Paul prayed in **Ephesians 1:18-19** that *'the eyes of your heart may be enlightened in order that you may know the hope to which he has called you, the riches of his glorious inheritance in the saints, and his incomparably great power for us who believe'*. I have shared with you in this book some of my failures as well as my successes and my tears as well as my joys. I pray that as you read and complete this book, God will use it to bring you closer and deeper into him.

3 Diving into the Depths of Christ's love

The depth of the Lord's love for me constantly amazes me. I know I'll never fully understand just how deep, wide, long and high is the love of God for the world, but I'm just so grateful that I've experienced it in my own life.

So many people think of God as a strict, hard and often sadistic person who sits in Heaven somewhere just waiting for an opportunity to hit you over the head and smash you down. That is so far from the truth. Someone once asked me in a school lesson, *"What is Hell like?"* I replied, *"Can you think of a time when you were very hurt? Can you think of a time when you were really scared and fearful? Then multiply that pain, hurt, fear, etc., by thousands of times and you'll begin to see just a little of what Hell is like."* Similarly, if you can imagine yourself at your most happy, most secure, most joyful and most peaceful and multiply that by thousands of times, then that will give you a little indication of what God in his incredible love has planned for you and me.

I was brought up by my parents to enjoy and experience the love of God and to recognise that Jesus was someone who wanted to be my best friend. God broke into my life very dramatically when I was only six years of age. My parents took me to a Brethren church where every Sunday I heard how Jesus had died for me.

One day I asked my dad if I could become a Christian. He

looked down at his six-year-old daughter and wondered if I really knew what I was doing. He explained to me very gently that perhaps I should wait until I was older before making such a big decision. I accepted his advice, but our Father in Heaven thought otherwise.

One Sunday night whilst dad was putting my brother to bed and my mum was out at church, I was standing in our lounge, not thinking about Christianity, when I had an amazing experience. I suddenly lost the power in my legs and fell to the floor in front of the couch on my knees. I didn't understand what was happening to me. Although I was confused, I wasn't frightened. I tried to get up, but couldn't. I was exhausted from trying, so I laid my head down on the couch to gather my strength. After a few seconds I tried to lift my head and found that was impossible also. It was as if a huge hand had been placed over the back of my legs and a huge hand over the back of my neck. Suddenly I realised I was in a praying position. This was the way I had been taught to pray every night beside my bed. I knew the Lord was speaking to me and that he wanted me to become a Christian but I didn't know how to, so I said my first ever *real prayer* which was, *"Dear God, I'll tell my daddy."* Immediately the pressure lifted and I was able to stand.

My father entered the room a few seconds later and I told him exactly what had happened. He then explained to me how to become a Christian and led me step by step through a simple prayer. The joy that flooded my being was quite incredible, I had never been so happy! That night I could hardly sleep and I jumped up and down on my bed in sheer delight and excitement at knowing and experiencing God's love in my life.

The more I've gone on in life the more I've discovered that his love is inexhaustible. I've let him down many times but he's never let me down. He's always there helping and encouraging me. Sometimes when we're going through a really tough time, it's not always easy to see God in it at all. Sometimes we *feel* he has left us alone or has turned his back on us - but God never does. I'm constantly amazed by how deceptive our feelings can be.

We must learn to put our faith in the facts (God's word) rather than in our feelings. If we put our faith in our feelings then our spiritual life will go up and down. One morning we wake up feeling good and we *feel* God loves us - the next day we wake up feeling miserable and we *feel* God is nowhere to be seen. God's word says, *'Never will I leave you, never will I forsake you'* (**Hebrews 13:5**). God's word is truth. What are you going to put your faith in - your feelings or God's word?

As I mentioned in the exercises in Chapter 2, I often encourage people to write a psalm when I am leading a spiritual exercise workshop. The initial reactions from people can sometimes be interesting, if not humorous. People begin to relax when they realise that all of us can express ourselves in this way; all you need is a willing and praising heart. You don't have to be a songwriter or poet.

One year when I did this exercise with a group of people in Switzerland, one person wrote a psalm that spoke about 'diving into a sea of God's love'. That phrase inspired us so much that Ray together with others wrote a song out of it.

SEA OF LOVE

I feel like I'm dreaming
Every time I think of you
I feel I'm in Heaven
Every day
Your love and understanding
In my life
Your loving is eternal
Everything to me.

Swimming in the sea of love
In the depth of love
Swimming in the sea of love
Deeper into Him

Waves of love surround me
I can feel your healing touch
Nowhere Lord to run to
Without you
Your heart is like an ocean
All I need
Your arms are always open
Holding on to me.

Robbie Bronnimman, Ray Goudie, Zarc Porter.

Copyright 1994 Integrity/Hosanna! Music/New Generation Music

If you've never experienced God's love or need to experience it much more deeply, then can I encourage you to dive into God's love? He will never let you down. Don't allow hurts and fears from the past to stop you going deeper into his love. (See Chapter 7 Dealing with Rejection and Fear.)

I've counselled many people who have been hurt or abused by others. Some have been hurt deeply by wounding words whilst others have been physically or sexually abused. When others have crushed you, it's often easy to reject all love, including God's love, in order to protect yourself. This is so understandable, yet you are shutting out the only person who can really help you through the hurt and pain.

Quite a number of the young people who have been in our teams have been abused in the past. One particular girl was physically and sexually abused which left her with deep insecurity. When I first came into contact with her she would hardly look at you. She stared at her feet and was constantly asking for affirmation. It was only as she began to experience God's love for herself that she began to be healed. We asked her to come and live with us, and during the first few months encouraged her to speak out her forgiveness to those who had hurt her. Now, many years later, you would never know she was the same person. Her whole personality blossomed as she began to experience freedom from the hurts and pains she had carried for so long. As she stayed in our home, she began to recognise that God loved her unconditionally and began to experience that love and acceptance for herself more and more.

What an amazing God we have! He never exhausts his love for us - he always has more. We can block Him through sin, unforgiveness or apathy, but despite this, he is always there to forgive us and lead us deeper into him. After many years of knowing him, all I can say is I love him and want to know him more. God loves each of us fully and unconditionally. He loves you whether you are a Christian or not. You only have to look at what he was prepared to do at the cross to begin to discover the depth of his love for each of us. My prayer for you is that this week you will not only discover the truth about God's love, but that you will experience a fresh touch from God as you dive into the depths of Christ's love.

———

VERSE FOR THE WEEK
'But God demonstrates his own love for us in this:
While we were still sinners, Christ died for us'
Romans 5:8

———

Day 1

5 mins   Write down your aims for this week. What would you like to see God do in you this week?

10 mins   Read **Psalm 146**. Write down what God says to you through this psalm.

10 mins   Paraphrase and memorise **Psalm 103:11**

5 mins   Spend the remaining time praying - asking God to reveal to you much more of his deep love. Ask him for revelation this week of how much he loves you.

Day 2

20 mins   Answer the following questions:

1. What is love?
2. How should love act? See **1 Corinthians 13**.
3. Write down ways of expressing love.
4. How would you sense that someone loves you?
5. Be honest, how do you treat those you love?
6. Does it match up to **1 Corinthians 13**?
7. Have you ever failed to love someone as you ought? Spend a few minutes asking God to forgive you for the times you have not loved others as you should. Ask him to help you love the way he does.
8. How did God show his love for us? (See **1 John 4:9**.)
9. What is the difference between God's standard of love and the world's view of love?

Write down what you can learn from your answers. Also, write down ways in which you can express to God and to others how much you love them. Put those ways into practice in your life.

10 mins   Read **Luke 7:36-50**. What does God teach us from this passage about love? Write down what you discover.

Day 3

20 mins   BIBLE STUDY
           Read **John 1:1-18**

           1. Who is the Word?
           2. Why did Jesus come to this earth?
           3. Read verse **10**. Why did the world not
           recognise who Jesus is?
           4. Meditate on verse **12**. Write down what you
           receive from God.
           5. Paraphrase verse **14**.
           6. Read verse **16**. Write down what blessings
           you personally have received from God.
           7. Read verse **18**. Spend a few minutes asking
           Jesus to make his Father's love more known to
           you.

10 mins   Go out for a walk with God. Thank him as you
           walk for sending Jesus to this earth.

Day 4

20 mins	Spend a few minutes asking God to help you read the following familiar scripture with new eyes. Ask God to speak to you of his deep love for you through this passage.
	Read **John 18** and **19:1-37**. Write down anything he says to you.
10 mins	Spend the remaining time in worship before God. Thank him for Jesus and for his incredible love for you. Use various ways to express your worship to God. You will find a list of Biblical ways to worship in the Praise and Worship Workout in chapter 2.

Day 5

10 mins	Paraphrase **Romans 5:6-8**
20 mins	Write out in full the following scriptures:

1. **Joel 2:13**
2. **Romans 5:8**
3. **Romans 8:38-39**
4. **Ephesians 2:4-7**
5. **1 John 3:1**
6. **1 John 4:7-9**
7. **Jeremiah 31:3**

Write down what these verses teach us about God's love.

Day 6

10 mins   Read **Psalm 139**. Ask God to speak to you about his great love. Write down what you discover.

10 mins   Go out for a walk with God. First of all, thank him for all the love he has for you and then spend the rest of the time reviewing your memory verse (**Psalm 103:11**).

10 mins   Read **Ephesians 3:16-19**. Use Paul's prayer for the Ephesians as the basis for your prayer to God about his love for you, e.g., *'I pray that out of your glorious riches you may strengthen me with power through your Spirit in my inner being,'* etc. First of all, write it out and then read it aloud to God. Make it your personal prayer.

Day 7

10 mins   Ask God for a picture of how he sees you and how much he loves you. You may find God will guide you to a portion of scripture or give you a clear picture in your mind or may whisper something in your ear. Whatever way God speaks, do write down anything you see or hear.

10 mins   Write a psalm to God about his great love.

10 mins   Thank the Lord for all he's done this week to help you realise more of the depth of his love. Acknowledge that you can never fully explore the depths of his love because he loves you so much. Ask him to continue to help you experience more of his continual, faithful love.

4   Discovering who I am in Christ

One of the biggest surprises that Gideon had in his life was being addressed as a *'mighty warrior'* (**Judges 6:12**). God knew who Gideon was and how in the future he would lead Israel; however, Gideon perceived himself as a weakling rather than a warrior. Here's my paraphrase of verse **15**: *"Who am I that you should address me as a warrior? I'm sorry Lord, you are mistaken this time. Just take a good look at me and my family and you'll know you've made a mistake. A mighty warrior - no way!"* You can hear him laugh, can't you? And yet he goes on to trust in God and his word and becomes an incredible man of God whom God uses to destroy the enemy.

One of the biggest surprises of my life is that God should want to use me. After all, who am I that God should use me? Yet as I learned many years ago, it's not our ability that counts, it's our availability. God can take any of us and use us to do incredible things if we remain trusting and obedient to him. A verse that means a lot to me is **Philippians 4:13** which says, *'I can do everything through him who gives me strength.'* We may feel weak or insignificant, but with God's Spirit within us, we can do ALL things.

If you take a look at **Joshua 1** you will be amazed at how many times God says to Joshua to be strong and courageous. God knows we need encouragement to discover that in him we are strong. One of the areas where the enemy can destroy us is by telling us that we are weaklings or failures. *"Who do you think you are?"* he says. *"Do you imagine for one moment that anything you do will make a difference in this world?"* He tries his best to pull us down and often he succeeds because we believe his lies.

At the end of 1994, I attended the Evangelists' Conference in Britain, which was administrated by the Evangelical Alliance. During one of the meetings, an announcement was made that they were looking for nominees for the committee that oversaw the conference. Someone I didn't know approached me after the meeting and asked if he could put my name forward. I laughed! I thought he was joking until I suddenly realised he was serious. I told him that if he could get someone to second it, then I would allow him to put my name forward. Immediately, much to my surprise, one of his friends who was standing beside him said she would second it. So my name went forward as a nominee. I was a little embarrassed because each nominee had to be voted on to the committee by the conference. As I looked around the four hundred evangelists who were there, I realised that not a lot of people knew me. I had been friends with most of the leadership for years, however, I didn't know many of the delegates. I committed the whole situation to God in prayer. At the next meeting, each nominee was asked to introduce himself or herself and say a little about their ministry. I went up and spoke for a few minutes, and although I am used to speaking at large events when I got back to my seat the devil was right at my side. As clear as a bell, I heard him say to me, *"Just who do you think you are? Just have a look around the room. Who do you think will vote for you? What ministry do you have anyway? Do you think your preaching is effective? No way! You're a failure. There's no way God can use you."*

The trouble with the enemy is that he knows how little we think of ourselves and takes a little truth and adds his lies to it. I sat there thinking, *"That's true - who does know me here? There's no way people will vote for me. I shouldn't have allowed my name to go forward in the first place. Yes, you are right - I am a failure. How could I possibly think that anything I do could affect others for God? What ministry have I got anyway?"* I could feel myself sinking lower and lower as I began to believe the lies of the enemy. In my desperation, I called out to God to help me and said, *"Please stop this attack and send me your encouragement Lord."* I felt so low as I was being bombarded with feelings of failure again and again.

When the meeting finished a man approached me and said, *"I want to thank you for all the help you have given my son. He attended a Christian holiday camp where you and the rest of ngm were ministering. He is a completely changed person. He went to the camp lukewarm in his faith and came back red hot. There are two books beside his bed. One is his Bible and the other is your book, and he can't get enough of both of them."* I could hardly talk to the man because tears started to come to my eyes. A few minutes later a woman approached me and thanked me for my ministry as it had meant such a lot to her. On my way out of the meeting, another guy spoke to me and said, *"I'm here because of you."* I asked him what he meant and he told me that when Ray and I were touring the country with the presentation called *'The Great Awakening'*, he had responded to a call to full-time work and was now working in evangelism.

I was overwhelmed at God's grace to me in providing the encouragement I needed just at the right time. However, God doesn't always do that. Sometimes, in circumstances like this, we just have to rebuke the lies of the enemy and start quoting scripture at him and also to ourselves about who we are in Christ. We are *new* creations - the old has gone - the new has come (**2 Corinthians 5:17**). So often we listen to the voice of the enemy and believe his lies. We need to start seeing ourselves with the eyes of Jesus. We need to believe what the Bible tells us about ourselves. We are joint heirs with Christ (**Romans 8:17**). We are part of God's family (**John 1:12-13**). We have been chosen by God (**1 Peter 2:9**). I believe that it's important to speak to ourselves and remind ourselves of who we are in Christ.

There's a list of verses in this programme that tell us who we are in Christ. Use them each day or any time Satan tries to deceive you into believing you are a failure. Always remember that God's word is truth, but Satan's native language is lies (**John 8:44**). The more you reaffirm with scripture who you are in Christ, the easier it will be to accomplish God's destiny for your life. Jesus says in **John 8:32**, *'You will know the truth, and the truth will set you free.'* We need to grab hold of God's truth and believe it. That's one of the reasons why it is so important not only to know your Bible, but also to memorise it and meditate on it.

I left that meeting so encouraged and built up by God and surprise, surprise, I was elected to the Evangelists' Conference planning committee and it was my privilege to serve in that way for many years! Let's encourage ourselves by remembering that God sees us as mighty warriors like Gideon. Read the story in **Judges 6** and see for yourself how much God used Gideon to fight the enemy and lead a whole nation into victory.

VERSE FOR THE WEEK

'I can do everything through him who gives me strength'
Philippians 4:13

POSITIVE THOUGHT FOR THE WEEK

God loves to take ordinary people and do extraordinary
things through them.

————

Day 1

5 mins   At the beginning of this week, take five minutes
to pray and lay down all the preconceived ideas
you may have as to who you are. Ask the Lord
to expand your mind this week to understand
more of who you are in Christ.

25 mins   Before we can understand who we are in Christ,
we need to understand who Christ is. Look up
the following verses and write them out in full:

1. **John 13:13**
2. **Romans 6:23**
3. **Colossians 1:15**
4. **Hebrews 4:14**
5. **1 Corinthians 2:8**
6. **John 3:16**
7. **John 14:6**
8. **Luke 1:32**
9. **John 6:35**

Beside each verse write what it tells you about who Christ is. Spend the rest of the time thanking God for who Jesus Christ is and for all he's done for you.

Day 2

20 mins   Answer the following questions:

1. Are you a confident person?
2. Do you find it easy/hard to believe in yourself?
3. When you set yourself a task to do, does it get done?
4. Do you feel uncomfortable with success?
5. How do you react to failure?
6. Are you able to receive a compliment from others, or do you immediately put yourself down?
7. If God were to ask you to do something for him how would you feel? Analyse and write down why you respond as you do.

10 mins   Read and meditate on **Isaiah 43:18-19**. Write down what you receive from God.

Day 3

30 mins   BIBLE STUDY

Read **Ephesians 2**.

1. The first three verses tell us what we were like before we came to know God. Write down each phrase that expresses what we were like, e.g. *'dead in your transgressions and sins'*.
2. Write down what God has done for us. See verses **4-7** and verses **11-22**.
3. Verse **6** says that God has raised us up with Christ. Write down how that makes you feel.
4. Memorise **Ephesians 2:8-9**
5. Meditate on verse **10**. Write down what you receive from God.
6. Spend the remaining time in prayer, thanking God for your place in Christ. Thank him for all he's done for you. Base your prayer on verses **4-7** and **11-22**.

Day 4

15 mins   Read **Psalm 8**. Write down what God says to you through this psalm.

15 mins   Spend this time in energetic praise, thanking God and praising him for:

1. Who he is.
2. Who you are in Christ.
3. Loving us deeply even though we are formed from dust! Speak out your praises to God.

Day 5

30 mins   Look up the following scriptures and write down what it says we have and are in Christ:

1. **Romans 5:1** - e.g., *'We have been justified through faith, we have peace with God through our Lord Jesus Christ.'*
2. **Ephesians 1:4**
3. **Ephesians 1:5**
4. **Ephesians 1:7**
5. **Ephesians 1:11**
6. **Ephesians 2:4-5**
7. **Ephesians 2:6**
8. **Ephesians 2:10**
9. **Colossians 1:2**
10. **Colossians 2:13-14**
11. **Colossians 3:3**
12. **Titus 3:5-7**
13. **2 Corinthians 5:21**

Once you have written each statement, read it aloud. Take time to thank God for each thing he's done for you. Make it your practice to read this list aloud regularly.

Day 6

10 Mins   Go for a walk with God. Memorise **Ephesians 3:12** as you walk.

20 mins   Read **Hebrews** chapter **1** and **2:1-9**. **James 4:8** says. *'Come near to God and he will come near to you.'* Imagine yourself approaching the throne-room of God. How do you feel - confident in Christ, or unworthy? Look up **Hebrews 4:16**. Thank the Lord Jesus for giving us access to the Father. Remind yourself that you have access to the Father because of what Jesus has done for you (see **Ephesians 2:18**). If you still feel unworthy, then rebuke the enemy. Agree with him that in yourself you are unworthy - but speak out that in Christ you have been blessed with every spiritual blessing (see **Ephesians 1:3**).

Continue to see yourself draw near to your Heavenly Father. Imagine yourself before his throne. Tell him your innermost thoughts. Talk intimately with him and tell him you love him. Hear him tell you how much he loves you and how special you are to him. Write down how you feel and anything God says to you.

Day 7

5 mins   Revise your memory verses - **Ephesians 3:12** and **Ephesians 2:8-9**.

5 mins   Paraphrase **2 Corinthians 5:17**.

10 mins   Read and meditate on **2 Timothy 4:8**. Write down what God reveals to you through this scripture.

10 mins   Read out your list of positive statements/ scriptures again. Write down all you have learned this week. Thank God for his love and goodness to you. Thank him for who you are in Christ. Ask him to bring these verses to your mind when the enemy comes to condemn you. Thank him there is no condemnation in Christ Jesus (**Romans 8:1-2**).

5   Developing a Praising Heart

One of the stories in the Old Testament that has meant a lot to me over the years is the story of the battle of Jehoshaphat against Moab and Ammon in **2 Chronicles 20**. Here was Jehoshaphat at war against a vast army (see **2 Chronicles 20:2**). As you can imagine, he is alarmed and calls all of Judah to fast and seek the Lord. Jehoshaphat knew he could not defeat the enemy on his own, he needed God's help and strength. He knew God was bigger than the enemy because you see he had a correct picture in his mind of God.

Sometimes, our problems seem so big that they overpower us and weigh us down and that's when it's difficult to have a praising heart. I know it's happened to me many times when my problems seem so huge. I've had to pull myself back to focus on God and his word, and when I do, suddenly my picture of God and his amazing strength and power increases and my problems, in the light of a BIG God, seem so much smaller.

We must begin to see God for who he is - a BIG God with incredible power and authority. He is our Heavenly Father who loves us and has our best interests at heart. Take a good look at God and in the light of that picture then take a look at your problem. Jehoshaphat went to his BIG God and sought him for instructions as to how to deal with the problem of this vast army. God speaks and tells him, *"The battle is not yours - it's mine and I will fight it for you"* (my paraphrase). Jehoshaphat immediately praises and worships God. His problem was still in front of him - nothing had changed, the enemy was still there - but God had spoken and Jehoshaphat believed him. The battle was the Lord's, not Jehoshaphat's, and the enemy was no problem for God.

It's so important to hear God's voice in the midst of conflict, because that releases you to praise God through the difficult times. The next day Jehoshaphat sent out the singers at the head of his army to praise God. In the middle of the conflict and the fear, they praised God, and it says in **2 Chronicles 20:22** that *'as they began to sing and praise, the Lord set ambushes against [the enemy] and they were defeated.'* They praised their way through the problems. Hallelujah!

There was a time in my life when I had to put this into practice for myself. Many years ago my husband Ray, went through a real crises in his Christian walk. He came to me one day and told me he was giving up Christianity. I was five years married to him at the time, and I looked on him as the spiritual leader in our home. Unknown to me however, Ray was living in defeat in his walk with God and he felt he could no longer go on living a life as a hypocrite. He decided the Christian life was not for him.

As you can imagine, I was devastated. I loved Ray with all my heart, yet I had always loved God. I could see if Ray gave up his faith, then we would begin to take separate paths in life and that could lead us away from one another. I knew I had a choice to make. I could either give up my relationship with God and go with Ray, thus saving our marriage, or I could trust God for Ray and pray that somehow God would do something that would change this situation. It was at that moment that I knew although I loved Ray with every fibre of my being I loved God more. I had always wondered whether I truly did love God more than Ray, but now I was sure of my commitment and feelings. I was determined not to let God go until he had answered me about Ray.

Unknown to Ray, I poured out my heart to God for him. Although I was extremely upset and couldn't stop crying, I wouldn't stop praying until God answered, but unfortunately it seemed as though Heaven was closed. The verse that kept going round and round in my mind was **Luke 22:31**, *'Simon, Simon, Satan has asked to sift you as wheat. But I have prayed for you.'* I felt the enemy wanted to destroy Ray so I kept on praying for him.

The whole night and the next day passed without Heaven answering. Around five that evening, while I was still praying and crying, God finally answered. If he had spoken in an audible voice then I couldn't have heard him more clearly. He said, *"Nancy, don't cry any more. I have seen your tears and heard your prayers and I will answer them. If you could see now what I am going to do in Ray, you just wouldn't believe it. Instead of crying out to me for Ray, praise me for all I'm going to do."* Immediately, I stopped crying. I hadn't heard of people dancing before the Lord, but I certainly danced all around our front room. God had spoken and things were going to be OK.

Ray came back in from work about five minutes later, and in my enthusiasm I told him what God had said. The same cold look that I had seen the night before came back into his eyes as he said, *"Well, if God's going to do that, then he's going to have to do it, as I feel exactly the same as I did last night."* From that moment on, unknown to Ray, I spent time praising God every day for what he was going to do in him, even though I couldn't see it. It was really difficult at times. There were times when I felt angry with God. I remember hitting the pillow one night as I shouted at God, *"Lord, when are you going to fulfil what you have said?"* Then I would repent before God, telling him that I trusted him to do it in his own time. It was only much later that I realised that from the moment God had spoken, he had begun working behind the scenes, but I didn't realise it. It was only as I praised God every day that it allowed God to continue to work in the situation. I didn't see even a glimmer of hope until about seven months later and then I could see some of the things that God was beginning to do; however, it was exactly a year later when God broke into Ray's life and began to fulfil all that he had promised me.

It is difficult to praise God through the difficult dark periods of our lives, but as we do so, God will bring his victory into our lives. Not only did God change Ray, but as I spent more time with God every day, my relationship with God also developed and deepened. As it says in **2 Corinthians 4:18**, let's *'fix our eyes not on what is seen, but on what is unseen. For what is seen is temporary, but what is unseen is eternal.'* Let's develop more of a praising heart. Let's see the enemy routed from our lives through praise!

VERSE FOR THE WEEK

'Don't worry about anything; instead, pray about every-thing; tell God your needs and don't forget to thank him for his answers'
Philippians 4:6 (The Living Bible)

Day 1

10 mins Read **Psalm 103**. Write down what you receive from God through this passage.

10 mins Write a list of all the things that have happened to you for which you can be thankful to God.

Go through each situation above in prayer and thank God for his love and care. Ask him to develop a thankful, praising heart within you this week.

10 mins Write down every worry and concern in your life right now. Imagine yourself coming into God's throne-room carrying a tray or a sack full of your worries. Lay them down at the feet of Jesus. Give him each one and see him pick each one up. Ask him for his peace. Lose yourself in praise and worship, thanking God for being in control of all that concerns you. Walk away without the tray/sack, leaving your burdens with Jesus.

Day 2

Read **Philippians 1**, then answer the following questions:

1. Who wrote this book?
2. In what circumstances did he write it?
3. What is the main theme of this chapter?
4. What happened when the writer first visited Philippi? (See **Acts 16**.)
5. What is the writer's relationship like with the church at Philippi? (See verses **3-11**.)
6. Read verse **12** - what has happened to him and how has it 'served to advance the gospel'?
7. The writer is obviously in prison for preaching the gospel. Imagine being locked up for years for a crime you didn't commit. Write down how you would imagine your feelings to be.
8. Write down how many times the writer uses the words 'rejoice', 'joy', 'thankfulness' and 'encouraged'.
9. Spend time asking God to develop a praising heart in you.

Day 3

15 mins   Read **Psalm 100**. Paraphrase this psalm. Write down what you can learn from what it says.

15 mins   Spend an energetic time of praise before God, thanking him for who he is, for what he's done for you and for his faithfulness throughout the generations. Using a praise song may help. You will find a list of Biblical ways to praise in the Praise and Worship Workout in chapter 2.

Day 4

5 mins   Read and meditate on **James 1:12**. Write down what you receive from the Lord.

5 mins   Memorise **James 1:12**.

10 mins   Go out for a walk with God. Thank him for all you see around you. Thank him for all the blessings he's given you, e.g. your family, home, job, church, etc. During your walk revise your memory verse (**James 1:12**).

10 mins   Read **Psalm 100** again. Then write your own psalm of thankfulness to God.

Day 5

20 mins   Read **Matthew 6:25-34**.

1. What does Jesus say we should not do if we are in need?
2. What is Jesus saying is God's heart for you?
3. What should we do if we are in need?
4. Repent of times when you have worried instead of trusting. Ask for forgiveness and for God to remind you of his word each time a worry or concern comes into your mind.
5. Meditate on verse **33**. Write down what God says.
6. Memorise verse **33**. Write it down on a card and take it with you wherever you go today.

10 mins   Read **Philippians 4: 6-7**. Intercede for anything that concerns you, remembering to follow the instructions in these verses. At the end, ask God to flood you with his peace!

Day 6

15 mins   Read **Psalm 46**. Write down what you believe God is saying through this psalm.

15 mins   Go for a walk. As you walk with God, thank him for all his love and care. Praise him for who he is and the fact that he loves you abundantly, completely and unconditionally! Also revise your memory verses (**James 1:12** and **Matthew 6:33**).

Day 7

20 mins   Answer the following questions:

1. Think through the whole week. Has it been easy/hard to develop a praising heart and attitude?
2. Are you normally a positive or negative person? Do you normally look for the good or do you normally expect the worst?
3. Analyse and write down how it makes you feel when you are positive.
4. Based on your answers above, ask God to make you aware of when you are being negative. Spend time asking God to help you have a thankful, praising heart.
5. What improvements, if any, have you seen in yourself this week?

10 mins   Spend time praising God. Tell him you love him and thank him for loving you. Praise him for your family and friends. Tell him you are determined to dwell on the positives in life - the things that are of good report. Write down all the positive things God has done for you this week. Praise him for all the good things he's done for you throughout your life.

6 Growing in Faith and Trust

I suppose if I were to ask you if you had faith in God, your answer would be yes. If we are Christians, then at some point in our life we put our faith and trust in a God we couldn't see but we knew was alive. However, our faith and trust in God should grow and develop as the years go by. It's often easy to trust God when everything is going well, but so much more difficult when there's hardship and problems around. I've found in my experience that God deals with us very gently and takes us gradually through the school of learning to trust in him, in order to build up our faith in him. If we learn to trust through each experience, then I believe when it comes to tougher situations, our faith has been built to believe God for more.

I remember one of the very first times God taught me to trust him for finance. We were still living in Scotland at this time, and Ray was in Canada touring with a Christian band. In chapter 11, 'Discovering God's plan for your life', I mentioned that whilst Ray was in Canada, God had been doing amazing things with him and totally turned his life around. He phoned me one night to tell me what God had done that evening, totally forgetting about the time difference. He phoned at 11.00pm Canadian time, but of course it was 4.00am in Scotland! While he was on the phone, he asked if I would bring £50 with me when I went to Canada to see him the following week as his finances had run out.

As Ray had been away for four weeks, he was unaware that finances at home were extremely stretched. I came off the phone and thought, *"Well, Nancy, where are you going to get £50?"* I prayed and asked God to provide it and then remembered that a retired minister in our church had given me £10 to take to Ray. The next morning the post arrived and in it was an envelope that had been posted in London a couple of days earlier. At that time, we didn't know anyone in London and I wondered who could possibly be writing to us. I opened the envelope and inside there was no note, only four ten-pound postal orders made out to Ray and me! I was astonished! I still don't know to this day who posted it, but I am incredibly grateful to God for speaking to someone at the right time. I am really thankful that they were listening and that they responded to God and released the finance that Ray and I needed at that point in time. I dropped to my knees immediately and with tears of joy thanked and praised God for his love and his provision. That was the first time I had to trust God for finance and he made it very easy for me. If he had told me that in the future Ray and I would be 'living by faith' and totally dependent on him for finances both for ourselves and for the ministry of ngm, I would have said, *"No way, I don't have the faith for that,"* but slowly and surely God has continued to increase our faith and trust in him.

There have been situations where we have had to trust God even though it looked as though he was not listening or even paying attention. What do you do when circumstances seem to show that unless God steps in, there's no way out? When Moses led the Israelites out of Egypt, they arrived at the Red Sea to find no way across. When he saw the armies of the Egyptians approaching, he cried out to God to do something! He also had the

Israelites moaning and groaning at him, asking, *"Why did you bring us out here to die?"* (my paraphrase of **Exodus 14:11-12**). Moses did the only thing he could do - pray and trust in God! He had never seen or even heard of God parting a sea before. However, God told him to raise his staff and stretch out his hand over the sea and that he would make a path through the water for the Israelites (**Exodus 14:15-16**). I'm sure everyone must have thought Moses had gone off his head. Stretching his hand across a sea? What good was that going to do? The armies of Egypt were almost upon them and all he did was to hold his hand across the sea!

We often think miracles in the Bible took place immediately. Sometimes they did, but often it required faith and trust in God's word as people believed what he had said. Moses believed God's word and stood in faith throughout the whole night. He had to keep trusting God throughout the night and eventually God fulfilled his word by parting the Red Sea (**Exodus 14:21**). As we grow in faith and trust in God, he will expect us to be able to believe his word despite the circumstances around us. Throughout the years God has been teaching us so much in this area and through each testing time, our trust in him and his great love grows stronger and stronger. He often tests us but he has never let us down.

I remember through one testing time being really confused as to what God was doing. We had been in full-time Christian work for about three years when we felt God tell us to give away what to us was a considerable amount of money. After much prayer, we had told God that we would obey him even though it meant that we would have nothing to live on unless God provided in some miraculous way. A few nights after we had done this, we received a phone call to tell us that our main financial support from our church was going to be cut by ninety per cent to £40 per month. I couldn't believe it! What was God doing? How were we going to survive? How were we going to pay the mortgage, never mind eat? Was God trying to tell us something? Perhaps it was no longer right to be in full-time Christian work. To say we spent a rather sleepless night would be an understatement! I was very upset and both of us were incredibly worried. We prayed and asked God to help us understand what was happening to us.

The next morning, we phoned our friend and mentor Ken McGreavy, and asked if we could meet and pray with him and his wife, Hazel. As we travelled to their home in London, we put a teaching cassette on in our car by Floyd McClung of Youth with a Mission. In the tape, he talked about how sometimes when we go 'out on a limb for God' it's as if we look back and see the devil cutting off the branch. However, as we stand firm in God, when the devil finishes cutting off the branch, the tree falls down but the branch remains in the air. In other words, even through tough times, times where it looks like we are cornered and are going to be defeated, God is still in control and he can make the tree fall down and the branch remain in the air. We serve the God of the impossible! We knew this was God's word for us, and as we began to pray we heard God say to us, *"You have asked me many times to increase your faith and that is just what I am doing."* Suddenly, there was a joy and a lightness in our spirits. We prayed and asked God to help us trust him despite the circumstances.

When we arrived in London, we explained to Ken and Hazel what God had said and we praised God together for the release of peace we had received. Over the next few months, God didn't answer our prayers in the way we had expected. He didn't provide hundreds of pounds for us; instead he sold our home, which had been for sale for nine months, and provided us with a rent-free home for several months. During those months he gradually increased our financial support bit by bit. As it says in **1 Thessalonians 5:24**, *'The one who calls you is faithful and he will do it.'*

I remember another time when our faith in God was stretched again. We were praying and asking God what to do about our car, which we used consistently for our school missions. Our car was a rather beaten-up Ford Cortina that kept breaking down. It was really embarrassing! We would arrive at a school where we would do assemblies, classes and a lunchtime concert. When we finished we all piled in the van and the car and headed for our next venue. More often than not, we had to get out of the car and push it to get it started, much to the amusement of the watching school-kids!

During our times of prayer, Ray and I felt God tell us that he wanted to give us a brand new car. We were really excited. We shared what we felt God was saying with people we respected in God in order to check that we had heard God right. We began to pray for God to encourage us in our prayers by sending us a few gifts. A number of small gifts started coming in and our faith and trust grew a little more.

We prayed and asked God to help us sell our old car, as we were about to embark on a national tour with BYFC, which would mean our car hardly being used. We could barely contain our excitement when we sold it about a week or two later for the exact amount of money we had asked for. We even told the person who was buying our car all its faults, including the fact that it broke down each time it stopped, but he still wanted it! We felt that selling the car was a real miracle in itself and that encouraged us to believe God for more. Not only that, but some friends phoned us and offered us a loan of a car until we were able to purchase our own. We continued throughout the tour to pray for God's provision for a new car, and the money kept coming in. Then we received a gift of a thousand pounds from a very unexpected source specifically earmarked for our new car.

We then asked God for a business contact in order that they could help us get a good deal on a car. On the next section of the tour we stayed with some good friends of ours, Ian and Marjorie Frith. When we happened to mention that we were praying for someone who could help us get a brand new car for a very good price, they told us, much to our amazement, that they could help. They had a business deal with a local garage and could arrange to get us a brand new car for a much-reduced price. As God was continuing to answer our prayers, we looked into what kind of car we should buy. In the end we picked a Maestro, which would cost around five and a half thousand pounds. We already had three thousand five hundred, and so we continued to pray for a further two thousand pounds before ordering it. Another two weeks went by and some more gifts came in but we were still far from the total amount.

Our friend Ian phoned us one day and asked if he should go ahead and order the car. Whilst talking on the phone to Ian, Ray and I prayed and felt a release of faith and trust in our hearts to say 'yes'. We put the phone down and began to panic! Had we done the right thing? We'd ordered the car, but didn't have enough finance. We decided we could only trust God for the rest. The day came when Ray had to get on the train at Preston and travel to Birmingham to pick up the car. A few more hundred pounds had come in but not nearly enough to cover the whole bill.

We prayed and felt Ray should go and collect the car believing that God would somehow step in. While Ray travelled to Birmingham, I was at home having a long conversation with God. I felt God had let us down. Where was the rest of the money? Hadn't he told us he would give us a new car? I was angry with God and took it out on the carpet I was vacuuming at the time. I didn't realise it, but the enemy was undermining God's word again and again. If we look at scripture we will see that this is one of his tactics. In **Genesis 3** it tells us that the serpent kept saying to Eve in the Garden of Eden, 'Did God say...?'

I eventually sat down and asked God to speak to me. I opened my Bible and it fell open at **Matthew 19:26** and I read, *'With God all things are possible.'* Immediately I began repenting and apologised to God for not trusting him enough and told him I would continue to trust him. My Bible had fallen shut. I opened it again and this time it opened at **Mark 9:23** and I read, *'Everything is possible for him who believes.'* I would never advocate opening your Bible and taking potluck as it were, but God made these two verses stand out so boldly that I never saw anything else. I told God I would trust him to bring his word into being, and suddenly there was a lightness in my spirit. I was able to praise God despite the circumstances and believe him to work it all out.

While this was going on with me, Ray was travelling by

train to Birmingham. He had read these books about people needing finance from God, who suddenly met someone on a train or a bus who gave them the exact amount they needed. So, full of anticipation, he boarded his train for Birmingham and sat down and waited for his messenger from God! At the next station, a man got on and sat opposite Ray. He looked at Ray and said, *"Are you a Christian?"* Ray thought to himself, *"This is it!"* and started to imagine pound signs in his eyes before answering with a rather expectant, *"Yes"*. The man had noticed Ray's Youth for Christ sticker on his briefcase and chatted to him for ages about God, before getting off at the next station without giving him a penny! You can imagine how Ray felt at this point. Where was the money? He was getting rather nervous but felt that all he could do was to trust God to somehow work a miracle.

Ian met Ray at the railway station and took him to the garage to collect the car. Ray took out his cheque book to pay, praying that somehow God would enlarge what was in our bank account, when Ian said, *"Oh don't worry about that just yet. You don't have to pay for the car today. I'll send you the invoice in due course."* Relief flooded Ray's heart as he realised God had stepped in.

The more I've gone on with God, the more I have realised that my deadlines are not always the same as God's deadlines. A well-known speaker once said, *"Your faith walk begins when you think it should end."* We thought we had to pay the bill when we collected the car. God knew otherwise. Ray came home with a brand new car and we didn't need to pay a penny! When we paid the bill several months later, God had provided enough money to cover the cost of the car. That incident really taught us to trust

God and his word despite the outward circumstances. Ray and I had in our minds that God would work in a certain way and by a certain time, but we learned that God has many ways in which to meet our needs and that the key is our trust in him and his faithfulness.

I do pray that as you do this programme God will take you further along the road in your faith walk with him, whether it be for finance, healing, salvation for friends, family etc. Do remember, when you are on a faith walk with God, that it is important that you submit what you believe you are receiving from God to others who are mature in the Lord. It not only gives you a safeguard against deception, but also as we grow in trust and faith in God it is important to have people with you who can help you through the difficult times. I pray that your trust in God will grow and develop as God shows you more of himself day by day.

————

VERSES FOR THE WEEK
'You will keep in perfect peace him whose mind is stead-fast, because he trusts in you. Trust in the Lord for ever, for the Lord, the Lord, is the Rock eternal'
Isaiah 26:3-4

POSITIVE THOUGHT FOR THE WEEK
Keep growing in trust and walking with God. Dream BIG dreams as there is nothing that you and God cannot accomplish together.

————

Day 1

10 mins   Spend the first five minutes telling God of your desire to learn how to trust him more deeply. Ask him to teach you this week what it really means to trust and not doubt. Read **James 1:2-8**. Tell the Lord you want to grow in faith and not be someone who is double-minded and unstable in whatever you do, but someone who has a firm foundation.

10 mins   Read **1 Corinthians 1:4-9**. Paraphrase these verses.

10 mins   Go out for a walk with God and memorise **1 Corinthians 1:9** as you walk. Write it on a card so that you can take it with you and revise it during the day.

Day 2

25 mins   Jesus encourages us in **John 14:1** to *'Trust in God; trust also in me.'*

1. What does it mean to trust? Look it up in the dictionary and write down the meaning.
2. Write down situations and times in the past when you have trusted in God. What did you learn from that experience?
3. Write down situations and times in the past when you haven't trusted in God. What did you learn from that experience?
4. Have you ever felt that God has let you down? Why? Explain your feelings to God and ask him for a picture of how he saw that situation. Write down anything that God says to you.
5. Read **1 Thessalonians 5:24**. Can you believe this verse to be true for you and your circumstances? If not, why not?
6. Spend time asking God for forgiveness for any lack of trust on your part in the past. Tell him you are going to put your confidence and trust in him because 'he is faithful and he will do it'. Thank him that he will never let you down.

5 mins   Revise your memory verse (**1 Corinthians 1:9**).

Day 3

30 mins   BIBLE STUDY

Read **Genesis 15**, **16**, **17** and **21:1-7**. This is the story of Abraham and Sarah and their faith walk with God.

1. What are you trusting God for at this moment in time?
2. Abraham believed (chapter **15:6**) after hearing God's word to him (chapter **15:4-5**). It's so important to hear God's word in your situation. What has God said to you? Ask him to speak into your situation and let you hear his voice.
3. What was God's promise to Abraham? (Chapter **15**.)
4. How did Abraham and Sarah try to work out God's promise? What lessons can we learn from this?
5. Chapter **17**. God confirms his word to Abraham again and changes his name. What was the significance of this?
6. Read **Romans 4:18-21**. Abraham looked at his body and the body of his wife and reckoned they were as good as dead. From a human point of view it seemed impossible for God to do what he had said.
   a) Write down all the human feelings and emotions Abraham must have had.
   b) Can you identify with any of these?
   c) Abraham believed God's word *above* the circumstances. What can we learn from this?

7. How many years did it take for God to fulfil his promise? Spend time praising God that Abraham kept on trusting God even though it was difficult. Ask God to strengthen your faith walk with him and develop a deeper trust in him.

It is worth noting that even though Abraham did try and work out God's promise himself rather than waiting on God's timing (i.e. Ishmael - **Genesis 15**), the Lord glosses over his mistake when it comes to describing Abraham's faith in **Romans 4**. Therefore, there is no reason for our failures to put us off continuing to learn to trust God.

Day 4

10 mins   Meditate on **Isaiah 26:3-4**. Write down anything God says to you through these verses.

10 mins   Ask God how he feels about you. Write down any pictures, visions, feelings or words you may receive.

10 mins   Spend time praising God for how he sees you and who he is. Use various ways to express your praise to God. You will find a list of Biblical ways to worship God in the Praise and Worship Workout, chapter 2.

Day 5

10 mins   Read **Psalm 33**. Ask God to speak to you
through this psalm. Write down anything you
hear God saying to you.

20 mins   Look up the following scriptures to discover
what happened when people trusted in God.
Write down a short account of what happened
and what we can learn from each situation

1. **Daniel 3:8-30**
2. **2 Kings 18:5-8**
3. **Daniel 6:1-23**

Look up the following scriptures to discover
what happened when some people did not
trust in God. Write down a short account of
what happened and what we can learn from
each situation.

1. **Numbers 20:12**
2. **2 Kings 17:13-20**

Day 6

5 mins   Revise your memory verse (**1 Corinthians 1:9**).

10 mins   Read **Matthew 6:25-34**. Ask God to speak to you through this passage and write down what he says.

15 mins   Go out for a walk with God. Thank him for the beauty of his creation around you and thank him for the love and care he took in making it. Thank him that he knows when a sparrow falls to the ground. Ask him to expand your mind to help you understand how important you are to him.

Day 7

10 mins   Write a psalm to God on the subject of trust.

10 mins   Intercede and pray for friends/family who are going through tough times or who are finding it difficult to trust God. Ask God to give you some scriptures to encourage them. Make sure you give them a note of these scriptures as soon as you can.

10 mins   Write down what you feel you have learned this week on growing in trust with God. Thank God for his faithfulness and love to you personally. Ask him to help you put into practice what you have been reminded of or learned this week.

7 Dealing with Rejection and Fear

We all suffer from rejection and fear at some point in our lives, but it's how we deal with these things that's important. When we are rejected and hurt, it sometimes makes us want to hide away from others in order to try and protect ourselves, however, this will only allow the hurt to fester and get worse. There are very clear guidelines in scripture about how to deal with hurts and fears. **Matthew 6:14-15** tells us that we should forgive those who have hurt us. When we have been hurt really badly, it is often very difficult to forgive the offending person, however, as scripture points out, it is the way to receive healing ourselves. The person who suffers if we don't forgive is not the person we are struggling to forgive, but is ourselves. If we don't forgive those who have hurt us, then it quite clearly says in **Matthew 6:15** that our Heavenly Father will withhold his forgiveness from us. In other words, we end up being in a worse state than we were originally. We can easily get eaten up with bitterness and that can lead to ill health.

Many years ago, a friend of mine was diagnosed as having cancer of the colon. She is a Christian singer and along with her husband sings and preaches in various European countries. Just before they were due to travel to England, she was so ill that the doctors told her that if she made the journey, she would return in a wooden box. They immediately went to prayer and sought to hear from God. They also asked many friends and Christian leaders to pray.

They received a letter from a church who had been praying for her, which said that if she accepted God's forgiveness then that would release God's healing throughout her body. They also received another letter from a friend in Ireland, which said, *"I am the Lord who heals you."* It also said that God wanted to totally heal the cancer and in fact God would give her a brand new colon.

Some years earlier whilst praying, my friend had felt compelled by God to tell her husband of an incident that happened when she was eighteen. She had befriended a new Christian and in her enthusiasm to help him had naively got involved more intimately than she ought, and as a result ended up becoming pregnant. Her parents were devastated and because of her age and also the disgrace, a decision was made for her to have an abortion. She was told never to tell anyone and the whole situation was completely covered over.

She had lived with her guilty secret for years, and when God asked her to tell her husband, in fear and trembling she confessed her past. The fear that he would divorce her had kept her mouth shut for years. When she finally told her husband, he was sympathetic and totally supportive of her. However, although he had forgiven her, she still hadn't been able to forgive herself. After receiving these letters she knew that God was asking her to do just that. Once she spoke out her forgiveness to herself, her healing started and instead of returning home from England in a coffin, her health had steadily improved.

A couple of years after this, she gave her testimony in public and again, through bringing everything into the open, she felt the healing had been completed. When she went back for a check-up, the doctors were totally amazed to discover that there was not any of the usual scarring in the colon. It was as if she had a completely new colon. God had promised a new colon and complete healing if she would forgive herself. When she did, he kept his promise and the healing was complete. Since then she has not only enjoyed good health, but has also worked extensively for God in Europe for many years. It was only when she released the fear and pain and forgave herself that the Lord was able to heal her. Not all rejection and fear leads to ill health, but in this case it was the ground in my friend's life that allowed the illness to develop.

Many people tell me that they could never forgive those who have hurt them because they don't 'feel' forgiveness. God doesn't ask us to wait until we feel forgiveness before extending forgiveness - he commands us to do it. It is so important to speak out to God your forgiveness towards your abuser. You may not feel forgiveness, but speak it out anyway in sheer obedience to God's word and he will bring your feelings into order in due course.

I've also discovered, when I've been hurt deeply by someone else, that each time the past creeps into my mind, it's important to continue to speak out forgiveness. Many years ago, I was badly hurt by a close friend, but I recognised that unless I forgave her constantly I would end up with bitterness and resentment in my heart. It was only as I continued to forgive and did not allow my mind to dwell on unhelpful thoughts that I began to feel released from the pain.

The great thing is that Jesus can identify one hundred per cent with our hurt and pain. He was rejected so many times in his life. He was rejected by leaders (**Mark 8:31**); by his family (**John 7:5**); his friends (**Mark 14:50**); and by his disciples (**John 6:66**). **Isaiah 53:3** says, *'He was despised and rejected by men, a man of sorrows, and familiar with suffering.'* Yet on the cross he said, *"Father, forgive them, for they do not know what they are doing"* (**Luke 23:34**). If Jesus can forgive those who abused and rejected him, then so can we. It's the way to walk in freedom.

I will be praying that during this week you will discover a deeper revelation of the Father's love and acceptance in your life, which will drive out rejection. It's only as we learn how much God loves and accepts us that we will be able to continue to love and accept others. At one point in my life, I remember telling the Lord that I couldn't go on after I had been badly hurt by some friends. I told him, *"How can I continue to love them when I'm being hurt so badly by them?"* God immediately spoke to me and said, *"What if I said that to you every time you hurt me? You have the resources within you to continue to love despite the hurt you feel."* Even though I found it difficult, I discovered his words to be true. May God help you to discover the resources within you to love those who have hurt you.

I would encourage you to dig deep into God's love this week. Ask him to reveal more of his heart for you. The more I recognise that God loves me and accepts me just as I am, that then releases me to love others more. My prayer for you this week is the same as Paul prayed for the Ephesians in **Ephesians 3:17-19**, *'I pray that you, being rooted and established in love, may have power, together with all the saints, to grasp how wide and long and high and deep is the love of Christ, and to know this love that surpasses knowledge - that you may be filled to the measure* *of all the fullness of God.'* At some point in the week, you may want to ask a friend or leader you can trust to pray for you. Praying with someone about these things can be very helpful, but do remember we must also learn to walk day by day in God's love and forgiveness.

As well as knowing how to deal with rejection in ourselves, we also need to be careful that we don't reject others by what we do or say. Many years ago we knew a fifteen-year-old boy who through a meeting held in our home became a Christian. His whole life changed completely when he discovered Jesus to be real. He couldn't get enough opportunities of telling others about his best friend. His ambition was to be a preacher like Billy Graham.

He gave his testimony at a young people's meeting and happened to say that he was now 'open to the Holy Spirit working in his life'. The particular church where he was sharing had, in previous years, gone through a split because of charismatic issues. When the young lad mentioned in his talk that he was 'open to the Spirit', the minister immediately stood up and there and then challenged him as to where in the Bible did it say that you were to be 'open to the Spirit'. He publicly rebuked this young lad and caused him a great deal of hurt and pain, so much so that the 'fire' that had started in him was almost totally snuffed out. This incident caused this young lad to withdraw and stop sharing his testimony in public. We need to be so careful what we say to others. We can damage others so badly by our words.

After one of our meetings at a youth camp, a beautiful young girl came up to us and asked us if we would pray for her as she had anorexia nervosa. Ray felt he should ask her when it had first started and she told us it had happened when her teacher picked her out in the class and called her 'pear-shaped'. Although, I'm sure, the teacher did not mean any harm by her words, what she said was almost like a curse upon this young girl's life. Since that day, every time she looked at herself in the mirror she saw herself as being pear-shaped and thought she was ugly. She couldn't see for herself that she was a very attractive girl. We prayed and broke the curse of those words over her life and she was immediately healed. She wrote to us a year later to tell us that she had had no problems health wise since that day.

We grow enormously when we are in an environment of encouragement rather than discouragement. Our sons, Daniel and Aidan, know that Ray and myself love them unconditionally. When Daniel was a young boy he used to sing at the top of his voice and dance around the room. However, the minute someone else entered the room, the singing and dancing stopped. He was free to be himself when he was with us because he knows we love him, but when anyone else entered the room it restricted him because he was no longer in such a secure environment. It's just the same for us, isn't it? If we feel secure with others, it releases us to be ourselves. If we feel insecure then it restricts us. Let's determine that we will encourage others around us this week and use our words to build each other up in Christ.

One of the main reasons why we are sometimes afraid of giving ourselves to others is not because we are naturally shy, but usually because we deeply fear that others will reject us. The fear of being hurt, misunderstood, unappreciated or let down keeps many of us from getting involved with others. Instead of being able to give our love to others, our fear leads us to protect ourselves by holding back in the relationship. We play safe, but we disobey God's command to love others. In **John 15:12** Jesus says, *'My command is this: Love each other as I have loved you.'* **Romans 5:8** also tells us, *'But God demonstrates his own love for us in this: While we were still sinners, Christ died for us.'* In other words, he didn't wait until we loved him before he extended his love to us. He loved us from the beginning even when we didn't love him. What a challenge to us today!

Fear of man, heights, authority, death etc., can also restrict our walk with God and cause us to be ineffective in our lives. Many years ago, I knew a lady who was incredibly frightened by the thought of being involved in a nuclear war. She was so driven by her fear that she could hardly talk about anything else. She wouldn't even go on holiday because she didn't want to be away from her family when the war started. She tried to prepare herself for what she felt would be inevitable and because the fear was so real to her it made her very ill. She couldn't enjoy today because of what tomorrow might bring.

God wants us to be people who are not controlled by fear but trust him in all areas of our lives. Fear is the enemy of faith and can paralyse our belief in God. As we go through this week, let's analyse what fears, if any, we may have within us and let's ask for a deeper revelation of God's love which drives out all fear (see **1 John 4:18**).

VERSE FOR THE WEEK

'My command is this: Love each other as I have loved you'
John 15:12

———

Day 1

5 mins   At the beginning of this week ask God to draw close to you. Tell him you want to pull down any barriers to his love you may have within you. Ask him to reveal, expose and take away any rejection or fears you may have.

5 mins   Look up the word 'anxiety' in the dictionary. Write down its meaning. Look up the word 'trust' in the dictionary and write down its meaning. Which of the two meanings describes how you feel throughout day-to-day life?

10 mins   Read **Psalm 34**. Write down anything you receive from the Lord through the reading of this psalm.

10 mins   Paraphrase and memorise **Philippians 4:6**. Read **Philippians 4:7** and discover what happens when we follow the instructions of **Philippians 4:6**.

Day 2

30 mins   Answer the following questions:

1. Identify any areas in your life where you may be fearful.
2. Analyse why you are fearful.
3. Do you find it easy/hard to trust God? Why?
4. Do you find it easy/hard to trust others? Why?
5. Do you find it easy/hard to trust your leadership? Why?
6. Is there anyone who has caused you hurt and pain or grief that you have not forgiven?

Look up the following verses and write them out in full:

a) **1 John 1:9**
b) **Colossians 3:13**
c) **Luke 6:37**
d) **Matthew 6:14-15**
e) **Matthew 18:21-22**

What does God say to us through these verses about forgiving others?

God commands us to forgive, even when we don't feel forgiveness. He doesn't want us to wait until we 'feel' forgiveness, he tells us to forgive. Speak out your forgiveness for the people who have hurt you along life's way.

Don't worry about your feelings; God will honour your obedience and will bring your feelings into order in time. If you do this in all sincerity it will be a significant time in your spiritual growth.

Day 3

10 mins   Read **Proverbs 3:1-8**. Write down anything God says to you.

10 mins   Paraphrase verses **5** and **6**.

10 mins   Go for a walk with God. Ask God to fill you with his love and peace. Thank him that no matter how you feel, the truth is that God loves you with an unconditional love. Continue to speak out your forgiveness to those who have hurt you. Do this any time the hurt comes to mind. Ask God to bless those who have hurt you.

Day 4

10 mins   Revise your memory verse (**Philippians 4:6**). Find another verse that carries the same theme as **Philippians 4:6**. Write it down and paraphrase it.

10 mins   Meditate on **Isaiah 12:2-3**. Write down what you receive from the Lord. Imagine yourself coming before God in His throne-room. Kneel before him. Express your love to him. Thank him for who he is and for your salvation. Hear him ask you a few questions:

1. Do you love Jesus?
2. Do you trust Jesus?
3. If your answer was 'yes' to the above, would you still love and trust him in circumstances that you didn't understand? Have you ever had to do this?

Before you leave his presence, allow his love to drench you. Look up **Jeremiah 31:3** and hear the Lord say to you, *"I have loved you with an everlasting love; I have drawn you with loving-kindness."*

10 mins   Write a psalm to the Lord from the intimacy of your heart for him.

Day 5

10 mins   Answer the following questions. Find scripture
           to back up your answers:

           1. Why is Jesus trustworthy?
           2. Will Jesus ever let us down?
           3. How much does he love us?
           4. Does he count us as valuable?

           Thank him for the encouragement these verses
           bring.

10 mins   Ask God to tell you how much he loves you.
           Write down what he says or any scripture,
           pictures, visions you may receive.

10 mins   Express your praise to God. Thank him for
           all he means to you. Get excited about your
           relationship with Jesus. Use dance and other
           bodily movements to express your praise. You
           will find a Biblical list of ways to praise God in
           the Praise and Worship Workout in chapter 2.

Day 6

15 mins   Look up the list of fears you noted on the
           first day. Go through the list and discuss
           each one with God, Present your fear to God
           and see him remove it from you and put it to
           death! Ask him to help you trust him in all
           circumstances. Thank him that his perfect love
           casts out all fear (see **1 John 4:18**). Imagine
           yourself leaving your fears at the cross and
           walking away with Jesus in total freedom.

15 mins   Read **2 Kings 6:8-23**.

           1. Elisha's servant was full of fear when he saw
           the enemy surrounding him and Elisha. What
           did Elisha do to get rid of his servant's fear?
           2. What does this teach us when we are fearful?
           3. Read **Psalm 91:9-13**. Ask God to speak to
           you through these verses. Write down what
           God says.
           4. Spend some time praying, asking God to
           forgive you for the times you've been fearful
           and unaware of his vast army surrounding you.
           Thank him for the protection he provides for
           you every day.

Day 7

5 mins   Read **Ephesians 3:16-19** aloud to God as a personal prayer. Thank him for the depth of his love for you. Ask him to help you experience it more and more.

15 mins   BIBLE STUDY

Read **John 20:19-31**.

1. Write down how the disciples would have felt when Jesus was crucified.
2. Verse **19** says the doors were locked for fear of the Jews. Why were they afraid?
3. Verse **26** tells us that even though they had seen Jesus raised from the dead, they still had fear in their hearts. What happened to them to give them the boldness to speak out in **Acts 2**?
4. Confess your fears to the Lord - ask him to come and fill you with his Holy Spirit. Pray for God to release boldness to you. Also pray for his continued anointing upon your life.

10 mins   Go for a walk with God. Thank him for all he's done in you this week. Ask him to remind you of the truths you have learned each time you feel rejected, insecure or fearful. Revise your memory verse as you walk (**Philippians 4:6**). Also thank and praise him for the truth of his word.

8   Dealing with Disappointment

Disappointment is something we will all experience at some point in our lives. Others will, at times, let us down and fail us even though that may not have been their intention. We may even feel disappointed in ourselves at times. I know I have felt disappointed in myself when I have reacted to a situation in a wrong way. Sometimes, instead of reacting in love, I have responded out of stress and tension and said something I never meant to say. Immediately, disappointment and failure creep in and then the enemy plays on it and it's easy to feel condemned.

Another area that can lead to disappointment is when we've been praying for something and it hasn't happened and we end up feeling disappointed in God. Does He not care? Is He not listening to my prayers? Where were you God, when I needed you? Many factors can contribute to us feeling disappointed, but it's how we deal with it that matters.

There's a story in the Bible that relates very much to this subject. Mary, Martha and Lazarus were very close to Jesus. They loved Him and valued his friendship very much, yet Mary and Martha must have been so disappointed in Jesus when he delayed his journey to them while their brother, Lazarus, was ill. **John 11:3** says that the sisters sent word to Jesus, saying, *"Lord, the one you love is sick."* They were desperate for Jesus to come and lay his hands on their brother, for they knew that if he did, then their brother would not die. Even though they had sent word to Jesus to come quickly, it says in verse **6** that he delayed his journey.

Can you imagine how Mary and Martha must have felt? I can just hear them saying, *"Where is Jesus? What can possibly be keeping him? Lazarus is going to die. Surely he'll come?"* They knew that the last time Jesus was in their area, the Jews had tried to stone him, but they thought, *"surely for one of his closest friends, he'll come! Where are you, Lord?"* Can you imagine how they felt when Lazarus died and Jesus did not even turn up for the funeral? Huge disappointment must have filled their hearts. Their brother had died and it looked as though Jesus did not even care.

When Jesus eventually arrived, Martha went to meet him and immediately said, *"If you had been here, my brother would not have died."* In other words, *"Where were you? Didn't you get my message?"* Mary then went to Jesus and she said the same to him. It says in verse **32**, *'If you had been here, my brother would not have died.'* You can just hear her saying, *"Can't you see we needed you?"* Even some of the people round about commented, in verse **37**, *'Could not he who opened the eyes of the blind man have kept this man from dying?'* It was loud and clear, *"Jesus, we're disappointed in you."*

However, Jesus asked for the stone across the tomb to be taken away, and immediately Martha says, *'But, Lord, by this time there is a bad odour, for he has been there four days.'* Jesus turns to her and says, *'Did I not tell you that if you believed, you would see the glory of God?'* In other words, *"Martha, even though you are disappointed, put your faith in me and you will see God's glory."* She obeyed Jesus and gave permission for the stone to be rolled away. When she did, Jesus raised her brother from the dead.

She could have stayed wallowing in her disappointment and allowed it to grow into bitterness against Jesus. Instead she obeyed his instructions and continued to put her faith in God. She didn't understand what was happening, but she trusted Jesus despite the awful circumstances. She did not remain in disappointment, but put her hope and faith in God, and as she did, it turned her disappointing situation into a victorious one.

Romans 5:5 says, *'And hope [in God] will not disappoint us.'* We may feel let down by others many times; however, are we going to allow the disappointments to lead us into bitterness and resentment, thus stopping the glory of God being revealed, or are we going to let it lead us into a deeper faith walk and a greater victory?

It encourages me to look at the life of Job, who even though he had been inflicted with ill health, bereavement, loss of wealth, in fact everything had been taken from him, yet he could say in **Job 13:15**, *'Though he slay me, yet will I hope in him.'* It doesn't matter who we are disappointed in, we need to deal with it by trusting God for the future. We mustn't allow disappointment to lead to bitterness and dryness, but allow disappointment to lead to greater trust and fruitfulness.

In 1987, together with the rest of Heartbeat, we released a single into the mainstream charts in Britain. We had felt very strongly that God had told us to be a voice through the media for him. We released a song called, 'Tears from Heaven' which got to number thirty-two in the BBC charts and number twenty-one in the independent charts. We appeared on Top of the Pops and were given incredible opportunities through the media to speak out for Jesus. In 1988 we felt we should release another single. However, this time the Church did not support the single as much as the first, and although this single was voted 'Hit pick of the week' by BBC Radio One we did not get any higher than number seventy. The media people couldn't believe it. They knew that we had been given incredible support the first time round and had expected that, because 'The Winner' was a better song, this one would break through to the top twenty.

Ray had put so much time and effort into this initiative, and when the single was not given enough backing, he was really disappointed. It really hit him hard and he felt that he had been let down badly by some of the Christian leaders, especially those that he had regarded as his friends. It was many months later, after carrying his disappointment for so long, that he finally got rid of the hurt he felt. At the Charismatic Leaders' conference, everyone was encouraged to write down their disappointments on a piece of paper, and once they had given them to God to throw them in a rubbish bin, signifying that they were gone for ever. Ray did that, and as he was praying and forgiving those who had disappointed him, Gerald Coates, a good friend of ours who had been very supportive of both releases, came up and prayed for Ray to be released from all the disappointments connected to the release of the single. Ray wept and wept before God as he released all the hurt and pain to him. Ray felt released from the disappointment from that time on.

It's so important to hand over our disappointments to God and to forgive those who have let us down. I'm sure you will find much healing through this simple act. Do remember that if we put our faith and trust in God, He will *never* let us down. **Deuteronomy 31:8** says, *'The Lord himself goes before you ... he will never leave you nor forsake you. Do not be afraid; do not be discouraged.'* In **Psalm 42**, David speaks to his soul and tells his soul to put its trust in God and praise God despite the circumstances. It's so important to speak to our souls and tell them to be lifted up. *'Why are you downcast, O my soul? Why so disturbed within me? Put your hope in God, for I will yet praise him, my Saviour and my God.'* We may not understand all God's will or ways, but we do know that he is a God who loves us immensely and constantly works for our good (**Romans 8:28**).

I am praying that as you work your way through this programme you will discover again for yourself just how committed the Lord is to you, and because of that, you will be refreshed, released and encouraged in him.

———

VERSE FOR THE WEEK
'The Lord is faithful to all his promises and loving towards all he has made'
Psalm 145:13b

———

Day 1

5 mins	Write down your aims for this week. What would you like God to do in you this week?
10 mins	Read **Psalm 145**. Write down what God says to you. When you finish ask the Holy Spirit to come with his healing and refreshment for you.
10 mins	List any areas where you have experienced disappointment in God, others, self, and present them before God in prayer. Tell God you don't fully understand why things like disappointment happen but that you want him to help you cope with the disappointments we all experience in life.
5 mins	Paraphrase **Psalm 145:14-16**.

Day 2

30 mins	BIBLE STUDY

Read **Genesis 37**.

1. Imagine yourself in Joseph's position. How would you have felt when all your brothers hated you and couldn't say a kind word to you? See verse **4**.
2. Did Joseph mean any harm to his father or brothers when he related the dream?
3. What did his brothers feel about him? See verse **11**.

4. How would Joseph feel at being ill-treated and put down a pit and then sold into slavery?

5. Read **Genesis 39**. Joseph had a dream from God but everything in his life was going wrong. How did he react? Did he react with bitterness, negativism, anger or did he serve God where he was? See **Genesis 39:2-4**

6. In the midst of temptation how did Joseph react and why? See verses **6-12**.

7. Joseph's dreams are again shattered. He is unjustly accused and ill-treated. How would you feel if this happened to you? How did Joseph react?

8. Was the Lord faithful to Joseph?

9. Read **Genesis 41**. Joseph was eventually made second in command of Egypt. God had fulfilled his dreams. In chapter **42** his brothers bowed down to him. What can we learn from the way Joseph dealt with disappointment?

Day 3

15 mins   Read **Psalm 22**. Write down any verses which God highlights. Ask God to speak to you through this chapter and write down what he says to you.

15 mins   Go for a walk with God. Memorise **Psalm 22:5** as you walk.

Day 4

15 mins   Bring a list of any disappointments you have experienced before God. Go through each one

and forgive each person who has disappointed you. Read **Colossians 3:13**; **Matthew 6:14-15** and **Matthew 18:35**. Speak out your forgiveness before God. Ask God to forgive you for any bad attitudes you may have had towards them. After praying, throw your list in the rubbish bin as a declaration that you have chosen to forgive. Any time you feel disappointment rising again, forgive them again. Pray for God's blessing to come upon them.

10 mins   Look up the following scriptures and write them out in full.

1. **Hebrews 10:22-23**
2. **Romans 8:28**
3. **Hebrews 6:10**
4. **James 4:8a**
5. **1 Thessalonians 5:24**

Ask God to speak to you through these verses and write down beside each one what he says.

5 mins   Answer the following questions:

1. Do you feel loved and accepted by God?
2. Do you feel loved and accepted by close friends?
3. Do you find it easy/hard to trust God? Give reasons.
4. Do you find it easy/hard to trust close friends? Give reasons.

Day 5

10 mins   List any promises God has given you that have
           not yet been fulfilled. Ask God if he wants to
           speak to you about any of these things. Write
           down what he says.

15 mins   Meditate on **1 Thessalonians 5:24** and **2
           Timothy 2:13**. Write down what you receive
           from God through these scriptures.

5 mins   Revise your memory verse (**Psalm 22:5**).

Day 6

15 mins   Use your imagination to see yourself coming
           into God's throne-room. Tell the Lord how
           much you love him and ask him to help you
           trust him more. Imagine yourself carrying
           your disappointments in one hand and God's
           promises to you in the other. See yourself hand
           over the disappointments to God. Imagine God
           taking them together with any wrong attitudes
           you may have had in the past, and throwing
           them into the deepest sea. Thank him that they
           have gone forever.

           Then hand over to the Lord his promises to
           you. See him gently take them from you.
           Thank him that he is faithful and even if you do
           not understand all that is happening, you will
           still trust in him. Hear him say that he loves you
           and hasn't forgotten you. Write down anything
           else he says.

10 mins   Read **Ephesians 1**.

Write out Paul's prayer for the Ephesians
and make it a personal prayer for yourself.
(**Ephesians 1:17-23**)

5 mins   Revise your memory verse (**Psalm 22:5**).

Day 7

10 mins   Meditate on **Romans 15:13** and write down
what you believe God is saying to you.

10 mins   Spend time praising and worshipping God.
Thank him that he is a God who can be trusted
and who will never let you down. Ask him to
forgive you for any time when you have allowed
circumstances to discourage you. Also ask him
to forgive you for doubting him and his love.
Tell him that he alone is worthy and that you
are glad to be in his family.   Perhaps try singing
out a new song of worship to God.

10 mins   Write down all you have learned this week. Go
out for a walk with God and thank him for all
he's done in you. Give yourself afresh to him
and tell him you will trust him for the future.
Hear him tell you that no matter what the
future holds, he will be with you and he will not
forsake you.

9   Knowing the Holy Spirit

I spent the first twenty-two years of my life going to a Brethren church and although I am very grateful for many of the things I was taught, I was given very little teaching on the Holy Spirit. My parents certainly believed in a supernatural God who was able to heal today and, in fact, my mum often received 'words of knowledge' from God which were incredibly accurate, even though she could never have known the circumstances other than by divine revelation. I grew up in an atmosphere where we expected God to speak to us, but it wasn't until I was in my twenties that God began to show me that I needed to be filled with his Spirit. Ray and I were married by this time and were actively seeking God about full-time Christian work. Clive Calver, who was the National Director of British Youth for Christ, had arranged to come north to our hometown of Ayr in Scotland to visit Ray, myself and our close friend, Sheila Walsh, to talk about the possibility of us joining BYFC.

During the day Ray, who was always interested in the theology of the baptism of the Holy Spirit, asked Clive question after question. I have to say although I was interested in what Clive was explaining about the Holy Spirit, I never really applied it to myself as I thought I had been filled with the Spirit at conversion. Towards the end of the evening, I went to the bathroom and while I was sitting there, minding my own business, God spoke to me! As clear as a bell, I heard God say, *"Ask Clive to pray for you."* I replied, *"But why, Lord?"* I'm sure the Lord must have thought I was really dumb. Clive had just spent hours and hours talking about the baptism of the Holy Spirit and here I was asking God, *"Why?"* God didn't answer that question, but just repeated the same request, *"Ask Clive to pray for you."* I argued back and forth with God telling him, *"Yes, Lord, I heard you the first time but please tell me why you want him to pray for me. Clive will immediately ask me, "What do you want me to pray for you?" and I will look a real idiot when I say, "I don't know""*. However, God just kept on insisting, *"Ask Clive to pray for you."*

After a considerable amount of time had passed, I felt I no longer could remain in the bathroom as I was sure Ray, Sheila and Clive would think I had fallen down the loo! As I walked back into the room, Sheila asked if I could drive her home as it was getting late. When we got in the car, I started to cry. I remember tears pouring down my cheeks as I told Sheila I didn't know why I was crying. I certainly didn't feel like crying, but here I was, in tears. I told her what God had said to me and she encouraged me to ask Clive to pray for me, as she felt he would be delighted to do so. On the way back in the car, I told God if he gave me the opportunity to ask Clive to pray for me then I would do it.

When I arrived home, I looked in the mirror and decided that no one would know I'd been crying. I was wrong! The moment I walked into the room, Clive and Ray immediately asked me, *"What's wrong?"* I knew this was God giving me an opportunity and so I blurted out that I believed God wanted me to ask Clive to pray for me. Instead of Clive asking me, *"Why?"* as I had anticipated, he immediately responded, *"That's great! God told me this afternoon that I had to pray for you."* Clive then laid his hands on me and prayed for me to be filled with the Spirit and then prophesied over me. A part of that prophecy, which has remained with me over the years, was that God would give me 'spiritual children' all across the land. I couldn't imagine at the time how that could happen, but after years of being involved in evangelism and counselling - God certainly has fulfilled his promise. Incredible peace and joy filled my whole being and I felt completely different when I went to bed that night.

The next day, during my special time with God, the Holy Spirit began to put strange words in my mouth. I had prayed for a year or two for tongues and nothing had happened - but here I was, speaking a small phrase over and over again. Was this the gift of tongues? Maybe I was just making it up - or perhaps, even worse, maybe it was the devil putting these words in my mouth. After struggling for a while, I began to realise that God only gives good gifts to his children and this really was a special gift from him. I now know that the enemy often puts doubts in people's minds at the beginning, confusing them as to whether this gift is of God or whether they are making it up themselves. In these circumstances, as someone once said, *"Doubt your doubts."* I have come to discover, over the years, that the gift of tongues is a really special and useful gift that not only builds us up personally but also is also essential in prayer and warfare.

There are so many people who are frightened by the Holy Spirit and by the gifts he brings. I'm sure the enemy knows just how essential the Holy Spirit and his gifts are to us, and so he tries his best to frighten us away. Recently, ngm held a national event called 'Shake the Nations' in Bristol. We received many letters afterwards telling us incredible things of what God had done during the event. God healed one particular person, even though no one had prayed for him. Another received the gift of tongues in the middle of the meeting. Some became Christians, whilst many others were restored or encouraged in their walk with God. However, amidst all the encouraging letters, we received two where we were told that some young people who came were really scared by the use of tongues in prayer. In fact, one person told Ray on the phone that all this praying in tongues *"scared the hell out of him."* Ray wasn't sure whether to rejoice or sympathise with him! People get frightened for many different reasons: lack of teaching, wrong concepts of God or bad experiences in the past, just to mention a few. **Ephesians 5:18** commands us to be filled (and keep on being filled) with the Holy Spirit. You may never have experienced being filled with God's Spirit, or perhaps you already have been filled at some point in your life. However, the question we should be asking ourselves is, *"Are we full of the Spirit now?"* I trust as you do this week's programme God will open up more the Holy Spirit's ministry to you.

————

VERSE FOR THE WEEK
'I baptise you with water for repentance. But after me will come one who is more powerful than I, whose sandals I am not fit to carry. He will baptise you with the Holy Spirit and with fire.'
John the Baptist speaking about Jesus in **Matthew 3:11**.

————

Day 1

5 mins   Write down what you are wanting God to do in you this week. Thank God for all he's going to do and say, and ask him to deeply affect your life.

10 mins   Read **Isaiah 40**. Write down in full any verses which speak to you and write down what God says.

10 mins   Look up the following scriptures and write down the titles (names) given to the Holy Spirit:

1. **Genesis 1:2**
2. **Isaiah 61:1**
3. **Matthew 10:20**
4. **John 14:17**
5. **John 14:26**
6. **Romans 1:4**
7. **Romans 8:9**
8. **Galatians 4:6**
9. **1 Peter 4:14**
10. **Psalm 51:11**
11. **Hebrews 9:14**

After reading all these scriptures - would you agree with the statement that the Holy Spirit is God?

5 mins   Thank God for the gift of his Holy Spirit. Ask the Holy Spirit to make himself known to you in a deeper way during the next few days.

Day 2

20 mins   We established yesterday that the Holy Spirit
           is God. Look up the following scriptures to
           discover a little of what he does. Write down
           each Holy Spirit activity.

           1. **Job 33:4**
           2. **Acts 9:31**
           3. **Romans 8:26**
           4. **John 16:8**
           5. **John 14:26**
           6. **Acts 2:4-5**
           7. **1 Corinthians 12:13**
           8. **Romans 15:16**
           9. **Acts 8:19**
           10. **John 16:13**
           11. **1 John 2:20**
           12. **1 Corinthians 12:1-11**

10 mins   Go for a walk with the Lord. Look for the Holy
           Spirit's handiwork in creation around you.
           Thank him for who he is and what he does as
           you walk. Ask the Lord to reveal more of the
           Holy Spirit and his work to you.

Day 3

10 mins   Meditate on **John 14:26**. Write down what you
           believe God is saying to you.

Read **Luke 11:1-13**

1. Do you have a hunger in your heart to learn how to pray more? Ask God to increase your level of hunger for Him.

2. What is Jesus' main teaching point in verses **5-10**?

3. Memorise verses **9** and **10**.

4. Paraphrase verses **11-13**.

5. Do you have any fear in you when it comes to giving the Holy Spirit control of your life? If so, try and analyse why.

6. According to verse **13**, will God ever give you a bad gift?

7. Take a few minutes to ask God to remove any fear from your life and increase your desire to allow his Holy Spirit to have more freedom within you.

Day 4

10 mins   Look up the following verses and write down what we should be careful not to do to the Holy Spirit.

1. **Isaiah 63:10**
2. **Ephesians 4:30**
3. **Acts 5:3**
4. **Psalm 106:33**
5. **Matthew 12:31**

Spend a few minutes telling the Holy Spirit you want to get to know him better. Ask him to forgive you for any time you have grieved Him.

20 mins Read **Ezekiel 47**. Write down any areas within your life that you know are dead or dry or need God's touch upon them. Put on some meditative music (I recommend my Meditation CDs 'Smile' or 'Meditations for the Beloved' both of which can be ordered by visiting **www.ngm.org.uk/shop**.)

Imagine God's Holy Spirit like a river flowing from Heaven to you. At first it is only a trickle but as you watch and pray and ask God to increase the power, the trickle turns into a stream, then the stream into a small river. The river looks crystal clear - it sparkles in the sun and seems to bring everything around it into life. Encouraged by what you see, again ask the Holy Spirit to increase his power and authority in your life. At that point ask God to remove any blockages in you to avoid the river being stopped. Confess any sin or areas of darkness (fear, hurt, etc) you know would be a blockage and ask God to reveal any area that you don't know about that would stop the Holy Spirit flowing freely in your life.

As you confess, begin to see the river increase in depth and width; instead of being a small river, it now turns into a vast deep river that no one could cross. Everything it touches comes alive - dead trees and plants spring back into life.

Ask the Holy Spirit to flood you and fill you and see all the dead/dry areas in your life come alive again. Speak life to your prayer life, your reading of scripture, your witnessing, your good works, your finances, your family, your church, your friends. In your imagination, see each area of your life come alive by the touch of the Holy Spirit.

Write down anything God says to you. Thank God for his river of life. Thank him for filling you full of his Holy Spirit.

Day 5

5 mins   Ask the Holy Spirit to continue to fill you full of him.

Again, use your imagination to see that river of his Spirit drench you totally. Commit yourself to going deeper with the Lord.

10 mins   Look up **Romans 12:6-8** and **1 Corinthians 12:4-11** and write down the gifts the Holy Spirit brings to us. Ask God to release more of his precious gifts in your life.

15 mins   Read, paraphrase and write out in full **James 1:17**.

Spend the remaining time thanking and praising God for the Holy Spirit and his gifts. Use bodily movements to praise God - don't restrict your praise to words only. You will find a list of Biblical ways to praise and worship God in the Praise and Worship Workout in Chapter 2. You may wish to use some worship music to help you.

Day 6

20 mins   BIBLE STUDY

Read **Luke 4:1-14**.

1. Verse **1** says that Jesus was *'led by the Holy Spirit'*. What does this mean and have you seen the Holy Spirit leading you in your life? If so, in what ways?

2. Is it wrong to be tempted by the devil?

3. What was the devil's aim in tempting Jesus?

4. How does Jesus deal with him?

5. Verse **1** says that Jesus was full of the Holy Spirit, and after fasting and seeking God he returned to Galilee in *'the power of the Spirit'* (verse **14**). Ask God if there's anything he wants you to do to have more of the power of God released in your life. Write down what he says and implement it as soon as possible.

10 mins   Go for a walk with God. Review your memory verses as you walk (**Luke 11:9-10**).

Day 7

10 mins   Read **Romans 8:1-27**. Thank God for the role
           of the Holy Spirit in your life. Ask God to speak
           to you through this chapter, then write down
           what you believe God has said to you.

10 mins   Write a psalm expressing your appreciation of
           the work of God in your life.

10 mins   Write down all that you have learned this week.
           Spend time thanking God for all he's done and
           all he's going to continue to do in and through
           you.

10 Discovering Angels

One of the subjects that is often neglected in Christian teaching is the ministry of angels. I haven't heard too many sermons on angels, although Billy Graham has written a very good instructive book on the subject. Nonetheless, you would have to go through your Bible with your eyes shut to miss the many references there are to angels and their ministry. Angels are mentioned in the Old and New Testaments nearly three hundred times. In the first two chapters of Luke alone, there are three separate occasions where angels appear on the earth. It is interesting to note that around the time of Jesus' birth and the beginning of his earthly ministry there was a lot of angelic activity, and this happened again around the time of his death and resurrection. It is fair to assume, therefore, that this will happen again when there is going to be a significant spiritual happening. It is encouraging to hear of stories of people who have encountered angels in these days.

I recently heard of a lady in America who tells the story of how angels protected her from a rapist. She was driving home late one night, when she heard an announcement over the radio warning people in the area in which she lived that a rapist had escaped from prison and had been seen in the vicinity. They gave a full description of the man and said he was very dangerous. She prayed and asked God to protect her as she travelled home. As she got out of her car, she thought she saw something move in the bushes. She cried out to God again as she hurried down the pathway to her home. As she approached the bushes, she saw the rapist hiding in them and realised that she had to walk right past him. Praying like crazy she walked quickly to her home got in the front door, and quickly and fearfully phoned the police. She was trembling all over. Minutes later the police arrived and promptly arrested the man. She asked the policeman if she could speak to the man, and she asked him why he did not attack her as she walked passed the bush. He replied, *"I wasn't going to touch you with those two big guys by your side."* The lady believes that the only explanation is that God sent his angels to protect her. What a comfort to know that God sends his angels to help and protect us.

There was a man in the Bible who was told by Jesus that he would experience an angelic visitation. In **John 1:43-51** we read of the conversion of Nathanael who became one of Christ's disciples. He was sitting under a tree one day, when Philip came along and told him that he had found the Messiah. Nathanael is sceptical but he decides to go along anyway and see this 'Messiah' for himself. When Jesus meets Nathanael he speaks as though he knows him, and tells him what he 'saw' him doing a few minutes earlier, and because of this Nathanael is convinced that this is the Christ. There is no other way that Jesus could know this information other than by divine revelation. Jesus then says to him, *"You believe because I told you I saw you under the fig tree. You shall see greater things than that. I tell you the truth, you shall see Heaven open, and the angels of God ascending and descending on the Son of Man."* What a promise!

Another person in scripture who saw angels ascending and descending from Heaven was Jacob. In **Genesis 28:10-17** it tells us that as he was lying asleep, God gave him a very vivid dream. He saw a ladder going from heaven to earth and the angels were ascending and descending on it. At the top of the ladder, he saw the Lord, who spoke to him and gave him a promise for the future. What an experience!

Just recently the Lord told my husband that he had been given two warrior angels. He remembers at the time thinking, *"I hope this doesn't mean I am going to go through a difficult battle at some point."* We never for a moment imagined the huge battle my husband was going to go through when he got ill and then discovered some months later that he had a tumour in his pancreas. He ended up getting his duodenum, gall bladder, a third of his pancreas and a little of his stomach removed and after the operation he ended up in Intensive Care for a long time. I was so comforted to remember that the Lord had given Ray two warrior angels. The story of what happened to Ray will need to remain for another day as we are, at the time of writing this book, still going through this huge adventure.

Although I have never seen an angel myself, the Bible does tell us that not only do they exist, but that sometimes they perform their tasks without showing themselves to be angels. **Hebrews 13:2** says, *'Do not forget to entertain strangers, for by so doing some people have entertained angels without knowing it.'*

Robin Knox who used to be in ngm some years ago told me a story of how he was carried by an angel when he was only a toddler. His family had just moved to a new area in Bristol when Robin's mum, Sheila, was told of a lovely walk by a river. She decided to try this walk on her way home from shopping and remembered that she was told she had to go through a gate to get to the path. However, when she reached there, she discovered that there were two gates. As she walked on, she decided that she must have picked the wrong gate. The pathway became rough and was less cultivated. It sloped down towards the river and after a while became very difficult to walk. She suddenly became aware that she was in a very dangerous position. Not only did she have her heavy shopping, but she also had Robin, a one-year-old toddler with her. She tried to go back up the slope, but found she could not. She was fearful of going on in case she and Robin landed in the river. She didn't know what to do.

She cried out to God to help her, and much to her amazement, just at that precise moment, a very big man dressed in fishermen's clothes and boots came up behind her and asked if she needed any help. She told him she was stuck and he immediately lifted Robin and the shopping in his arms. He told her to follow on behind him as he strode confidently towards safety. Sheila followed as best she could along the side of the river, holding on to branches or anything she could find to keep her from falling.

When she reached the other side, the man made sure she was okay before walking away. She discovered later that it was unusual to see a fisherman beside that particular river. Also, she could not believe how easy it had been to trust this man. She was not in the habit of giving her child to a complete stranger, but she felt she could trust him totally. Was this an angel sent by God to help Sheila and Robin exactly at the time they needed help? Sheila certainly feels this to be the case.

When Ray and I go away from home we never leave without asking God to send his angels to protect our possessions while we are gone. It's wonderful to realise that one of the functions of the angels is to protect us. **Psalm 91:11** says, *'He will command his angels concerning you to guard you in all your ways.'*

Although we don't normally *see* angels, we can see the result of their help. I remember my mum and dad phoning me a few years back to tell me of an incident which had happened to them. My mum had mislaid her wedding ring; although she remembered putting it on the dressing table in her bedroom, when she went to look for it, she couldn't find it anywhere. She and dad hunted the whole of the bedroom. They took everything off the dressing table and then put everything back, bit by bit. They searched everywhere for hours but could not find it. As you can imagine my mum was upset at the thought of losing her wedding ring, and before she went to bed that night she prayed again that God would somehow help her find it.

The next morning, as she was dressing, she noticed the ring sitting in the most prominent place on the dressing table. Both mum and dad know they could not have missed it the day before. It had not been there when they had hunted for it. The only explanation was that God had answered my mum's prayer by sending an angel to find the ring and put it where mum and dad would see it.

Although my parents shared that story with me, they hesitated to share it with anyone else in case they would not believe them, until they heard a missionary tell a similar story. She spoke of a time when she had lost some important keys and could not find them anywhere. At a later stage she found them in a place where she had looked several times. She said she knew an angel must have placed them there because she had looked in that particular place many times and knew she could not have missed them. It's brilliant to know that God is interested in every area of our lives and sends his angels to help us.

The world has a weird view of angels. Sometimes they are pictured as effeminate weirdos with beautiful wings and bowed heads, usually sitting on a cloud, strumming a harp and wearing a long white nightie, bored out of their minds. The Bible, however, does not picture them like that at all. In **Numbers 22:31** the angel of the Lord is pictured as a warrior.

Another myth that the world believes is that angels are humans who have died and gone to heaven. The Bible tells us quite clearly that as well as creating mankind, God created angels. In **Colossians 1:16** it tells us that all things, whether *'visible or invisible'*, were created by God.

The new age movement encourages people to find their 'inner spirit guide' or 'wise being within' or talk to their 'personal angel' to ask for help, support, love or direction. The Bible states quite clearly that we should not 'worship' angels but that we should 'worship the Lord God and serve him only'. **Matthew 4:10**. **Revelation 22:8-9** says *'I, John, am the one who heard and saw these things. And when I had heard and seen them, I fell down to worship at the feet of the angel who had been showing them to me. But he said, "Do not do it! I am a fellow servant with you and with your brothers the prophets and of all who keep the words of this book. Worship God!"'* There are great dangers in worshipping or trying to contact your personal 'inner spirit guide'. The only Spirit we should pursue with all our heart and mind is the Holy Spirit.

I pray that as you do this week's programme, you will discover for yourself more about the ministry of angels. We need to be more aware that even though we cannot see them, angelic forces are very real.

———

VERSE FOR THE WEEK

'Praise the Lord, you his angels, you mighty ones who do his bidding, who obey his word'
Psalm 103:20

———

Day 1

5 mins   Write down your aims and desires for this week as you go through this programme. Ask God to open your mind as you discover more about the supernatural. Ask God to take from you any preconceived ideas you may have about angels.

10 mins   Read **Psalm 91** and write down what you receive through this psalm from God.

5 mins   Write down your thoughts and perceptions about angels and ask God to confirm over the next few days if these are correct or incorrect.

10 mins   Go out for a walk with God and memorise **Psalm 91:11-12** as you walk. Thank God for the protection he gives you. Thank him for the ministry of angels. Ask him to remind you, even though you cannot see the angelic forces,

that there are many who are 'with' you.

Day 2

15 mins   Look up the following scriptures to discover the answers to the following questions:

1. Do angels speak? See **Luke 1:19**.
2. Are angels to be worshipped? See **Revelation 19:10**.
3. Do angels marry? See **Matthew 22:30**.
4. Is it possible for us to have 'guardian angels'? See **Matthew 18:10** and **Acts 12:15**.
5. Is it possible to meet an angel and not know it? See **Hebrews 13:2**.
6. Are angels sent to serve us? See **Hebrews 1:14**.
7. What do angels do when someone becomes a Christian? See **Luke 15:10**.

10 mins   Meditate on **Hebrews 1:3**. Write down what you receive from this verse.

5 mins   Revise your memory verses (**Psalm 91:11-12**).

Day 3

Read **Luke 1:5-25**.

1. What did it mean to Zechariah to be chosen to go into the temple and burn incense?
2. What was Zechariah's response at seeing an angel?
3. The angel brought good news to Zechariah and his wife Elizabeth, yet Zechariah met the news with unbelief. What happened to him because of that?
4. How much does unbelief play a part in your own life?

Read **Luke 1:26-38**

5. What was Mary's response at seeing an angel?
6. She asked questions, as Zechariah had done, but why was she not struck dumb?
7. Imagine and write down how Mary must have felt when she heard the angel's message. She was a young virgin   who was engaged to be married. She must have known that no one would believe the story that she got pregnant by the Holy Spirit.
8. Meditate on verse **38**. Write down what God says to you through this verse.

Day 4

15 mins   Paraphrase **Hebrews 2:5-9**.

15 mins   Spend time thanking God for sending Jesus
           to die on the cross for us. Thank him for his
           salvation plan for our lives. It is interesting to
           note that there is no salvation plan for angels
           - once an angel turns away from God, then he
           is automatically damned. Thank Jesus that he
           was willing to give up all that he had in Heaven
           for you. Thank him that he was willing to be
           made lower than the angels.

           Spend time worshipping him and thanking him
           for your salvation. Use some of the Biblical
           ways of worship mentioned in the Praise and
           Worship Workout in Chapter 2. Perhaps try
           some ways that you haven't used before.

Day 5

10 mins   Read **Luke 15:1-10**. Spend time praying to God
           about friends or family who do not yet know
           him. Ask the Lord if there is anything you can
           do which would help them come to know him.
           Follow any instructions God may give you. Ask
           the Lord to release his angels to help you do
           what he has asked you to do.

10 mins   Read **Revelation 22**. Write down what the Lord
           says to you through the reading of this chapter.
           Also, write down what this chapter teaches you
           about angels and their ministry.

10 mins   Look up the following scriptures to find out
            how angels helped Jesus in his ministry here on
            earth. Write your answers down.

            1. **Luke 2:10-12**
            2. **Matthew 4:11**
            3. **Luke 22:43**
            4. **Matthew 28:5-7**
            5. **Acts 1:9-11**

Day 6

10 mins   Read **2 Kings 6:8-23**. Write down what you can
            learn from these verses.

10 mins   Look up the following scriptures to discover
            what kind of ministry angels have been given in
            connection with Christians. Write down beside
            each verse what task angels had to carry out.

            1. **Genesis 24:7** and **40**
            2. **1 Kings 19:5-8**
            3. **Psalm 34:7**
            4. **Daniel 6:22**
            5. **Acts 12:7-10**
            6. **Matthew 24:31**

10 mins   Write a psalm to the Lord thanking him for all
            the love and help he gives us day by day.

Day 7

10 mins   Answer the following questions:

1. Have you experienced the ministry of angels at any time in the past? If yes, then write down what happened.
2. If not, then if an angel appeared before you how would you react?
3. Have you been involved at any time your past with occult or Satanic activity?
4. If yes, then have you renounced Satan and asked someone to pray with you? If your answer is no, then do make sure you see someone in church leadership to talk through what happened to you in the past.

Spend an energetic time praising God for what he means to you. Tell him how much you love him and ask him to take you deeper and show you more of who he is.

10 mins   Go out for a walk with God. Thank him for all his love for you and for the way he watches over you and cares for you. Revise your memory verses as you walk. (**Psalm 91:11-12**).

10 mins   Go over all your notes for this week. Write down a summary of what you have learned.

11 Discovering God's Plan for your Life

I've discovered, as I've gone deeper with God that everything we do in life is training for what lies ahead. I've also discovered that had I known what lay ahead I would have run a mile! In my younger years, I would never have imagined myself to be a preacher, yet here I am spending a lot of my time preaching and teaching at various meetings and events. The truth is that the first time I was on stage at a Christian event, I fell off it!

It was Unity's first booking in Scotland. Unity was a modern choir initiated by Ray and his brother Derek, and the first project we embarked upon was a presentation called 'Time for Christmas'. I had been asked to do some narration with a friend of mine called Frances. The lights came on us and as she uttered her first word, "Suddenly ...", I crossed my legs and discovered that my chair wasn't fully on the stage. Before she could say any more, both the chair and I promptly disappeared from view! The audience thought this was part of the show and fell about laughing.

In my first year with British Youth for Christ, while I was singing with Sheila Walsh, had anyone asked me to say anything publicly that wasn't scripted, you wouldn't have seen me for dust. My mum, like me, had been brought up in a Brethren church and because they did not allow women to speak in church, she was never encouraged to do any public speaking. At a Youth for Christ conference in Scotland, someone asked her to pray publicly. Afterwards, someone took her father aside and told him that his daughter had a real gift in communication from God and should be encouraged to use it. However, because of their Brethren roots, she was never allowed to do so. Although I was brought up in the Brethren church, my mum and dad had the insight to send me for elocution lessons. I was taught how to project my voice and how to speak in public. Eventually, I qualified as an Elocution teacher and throughout the years have used what I was taught to help others in the art of communication.

One day, many years ago while spending quality time with God, I felt that I should list any talents or gifts, however small or inadequate I thought they were, on a piece of paper, and offer them to God as a sacrifice. I remember writing down singing, public speaking (I used to say poetry), typing, etc., and then I presented each one before God. I thanked him for each gifting but told him that I voluntarily there and then would lay them down and unless God opened up opportunities for me, I would not push or strive to use them. I didn't feel particularly talented, however, I told him that if he opened up opportunities, then I would trust him and take them. I felt I was laying them on God's altar and if he chose to put them to death, then so be it. It reminded me a little of Abraham in **Genesis 22** when he was asked to offer Isaac as a burnt offering.

It wasn't until years later that I discovered how important my actions were at that time. Sometimes we trust in our abilities more than we trust in God, or sometimes our ability to do something becomes more important to us than our relationship with him. At other times we may feel that our gifts don't amount to very much and feel that God could never use them.

A couple of days later, after laying these things down, I received a phone call from a well-known evangelist, who asked me if I would sing on a national Christian tour called 'Our God Reigns' which would be touring for ten days at all the biggest theatres in the country, starting with three events at the Royal Albert Hall. I was asked to sing with Dave Pope, Graham Kendrick and Sheila Walsh. It was a real honour to be asked but I didn't feel capable or talented enough to be able to do it. However, because I had told God I would only use my gifts if he opened up the opportunities ... I gulped hard and said, *"yes"*. I'm sure my answer would have been quite different had I not had that special time with God.

When we joined BYFC later we prayed for musicians whose first love and passion was God. We wanted people who had 'died' to their music. In other words, music wasn't the most important thing in them, but God was. We wanted them to be professional and dedicated in their art form but the music wasn't to be the most important thing in their lives. When we interview people today for our music teams or for our Internship courses, this is still one of the main things we look for in those who want to work for God through music. I do believe if you lay down your talents/ gifts and trust God to raise them up rather than striving in your own strength, then God will honour you. I know if you do this, it will be a significant turning point in your life.

If you are asking God to confirm whether you should serve him in full-time Christian work, then again this programme will be very helpful. One of the things God did when he called Ray and me into full-time Christian work was to confirm his call over and over again. Ray was firmly established in his parents' business at the time, and although he had taken five months leave of absence to drum for Dave Pope in this country and in Canada, he had no intention of ever leaving the business. In fact, Ray and I had always said we never wanted to live anywhere else but Scotland. However, we hadn't planned for the voice of God breaking into our lives.

During Ray's time with Dave, several Christian leaders came and asked us if we had ever thought of working full-time for God. We hadn't really given it much thought, but at that time I began to seriously ask God if this could be right for us. One day, I felt God speak to me and give me an incredible peace in my heart that he was indeed calling us into full-time Christian work in the near future. As far as I was concerned God had spoken, therefore it would definitely happen, but Ray was much more cautious. He wanted to be absolutely sure that this was right. We continued to receive words from scripture that seemed to be pointing us in that direction, but Ray was concerned about his parents' shoe retail business. He didn't want to let his mum and dad down. At that point they wanted to open up another shop and put Ray in charge. How could he possibly tell them that he was thinking of moving away?

While in Canada, Ray attended a large church meeting and at the end an appeal was given for those who felt God was calling them into full-time work to stand. Ray at that time did not like responding to appeals, but felt the pull of God on his life. He stood along with hundreds of another people. Later, on his way out of the service, an older man whom he had never met came up and asked him if he felt that God was calling him into full-time work. Ray confirmed that this was so. The man went on to say, *"I felt God ask me to come and speak to you. Many years ago, God called me into full-time work, but because I was involved in my family business and I didn't want to let my parents down, I gave in to family pressure and didn't respond to God's calling. Now, twenty-five years later, I realise I disobeyed God. If this applies to you in any way, do not allow pressures to hold you back from what God wants to do with you."* Ray couldn't believe it, as it described his situation so clearly. Ray knew that God was speaking and that if he didn't do what God had told him to do, he would be living in disobedience.

When we came home from Canada, Clive Calver came up to see us in Ayr about the possibility of us joining British Youth for Christ. While he was with us, we prayed together and Clive gave us a prophecy. One of the things God said through the prophecy was, *"Do not worry about your loved ones, I will look after them - you follow after me."* **Psalm 37:4-6** was also quoted in the prophecy. Afterwards, Ray turned to me and said, *"Well, if that was God, I'd like him to confirm that."*

The next morning, a letter arrived from a friend who was in the Royal Navy. The letter had been written several weeks before, but in it he said, *"Ray, I feel I need to stop what I am saying and tell you something I believe God wants you to hear - in fact he may have told you this already."* He went on to quote the prophecy almost word for word and even used the same scriptures. Ray and I were so excited that God had confirmed the prophecy in such a special way. God was confirming over and over again that he wanted us to obey him and he would look after our loved ones.

We continued to receive confirmation after confirmation through scripture, through others, through our church leadership and through the peace in our hearts. However, it wasn't easy to obey God. It would have been much easier to succumb to the pressure to stay in Scotland, but we knew we couldn't disobey God.

It may be that through this programme you will feel the need to resubmit your life to Christ and that, through that decision, God may highlight a new, fresh calling on your life. God may want you to get involved in a particular area of your local church, or get involved more in your local community. It may be a move in your job or to serve him in some form of mission work at home or abroad. If you feel the Lord may be leading you to a particular area of work, then ask him to fan it into flame in yourself. If, indeed, it is just your own good idea, then it will fade away; however if it is God, then it will get stronger and stronger in you, as he confirms it again and again. It is wise in decisions like this to have your call confirmed by your church leadership. God will often confirm his calling by scripture, through your church leadership, through friends and through the peace in your heart.

Obviously timing is of prime importance. We need to hear God as to when he wants to bring his calling into fruition. We can learn so much from David in the Old Testament when he would not grab his destiny by killing Saul (see **1 Samuel 24**). He preferred to wait until God brought his purposes into being. I trust as you seek God for his calling on your life through this programme, that God will give you clarity and direction for the job that only you can do.

———

VERSE FOR THE WEEK

'Delight yourself in the Lord and he will give you the desires of your heart'

Psalm 37:4

POSITIVE STATEMENT FOR THE WEEK

'No eye has seen, nor ear has heard, no mind has conceived what God has prepared for those who love him'

1 Corinthians 2:9

———

Day 1

5 mins   Write out your aims for this week. What do you want to achieve? Spend time asking God to do the above.

20 mins   BIBLE STUDY

Read **John 15**

1. What does Jesus ask us to do in this chapter? List the things he calls us to do.
2. What must we do if we want to bear fruit in our lives? (See verses **4** and **5**.)
3. Write out every promise in this chapter.
4. Verse **16** says that Jesus chose us - spend a few minutes meditating on the fact that Jesus has chosen you. Write down how it makes you feel.

5. Note in verse **20** what Jesus says about persecution. Write down ways in which you could be persecuted in these days.
6. Spend time asking God to help you to accept persecution as well as blessing both now and in the future.

5 mins   Go out for a short walk with God. Thank him for his creation and the life he has given you. Express your desire to live your life for him.

Day 2

15 mins   We looked yesterday at the subject of persecution. Read **Mark 10:29-30** and **Matthew 5:11-12**.

1. What type of persecution have you experienced in your life (e.g., people speaking against you because of your faith etc.)?
2. How do you react when hard times and persecution come along?
3. Find a verse in scripture that tells you how you should react when you are being persecuted.

Spend time asking God to help you rejoice through hardship, pain and misunderstanding.

5 mins   Memorise **Matthew 5:11-12**

10 mins   Jesus goes on to say in verse **13** that we are the salt of the earth. Write down all the things that salt does, e.g., cleanses, purifies, etc. Salt

is essential for so many things. Jesus is saying that we are essential for his plans and purposes for this world. Write down how that makes you feel. Finish off by thanking God that you are special to him and his purposes.

Day 3

30 mins   BIBLE STUDY

Read **Genesis 22:1-19**.

1. Abraham had prayed for Isaac for many years. God had promised him a son and then in his old age (when he was a hundred years old) Isaac was born. All the promises of God were to be fulfilled through Isaac. Write down how Abraham must have felt when he heard God tell him to sacrifice him as a burnt offering.
2. Isaac was not told that he was going to be the sacrifice - write down how he must have felt when his father bound him and put him on the altar. What can we learn from this?
3. God was pleased with Abraham's obedience and response. What did God say and promise to Abraham (see verses **12** and **15-18**)?
4. List what are the most precious things in your life.
5. Paul says in **Philippians 3:4-11** that he considers his background (i.e. being a Pharisee, a Hebrew, knowing the law in detail, being intellectual etc.) rubbish in comparison to knowing Jesus. His background (before he became a Christian) was very special to him.

Abraham was willing to sacrifice his beloved son because he trusted God with everything he had. Would you be willing to trust the most precious thing you have to Jesus?

6. If you can, imagine yourself presenting that thing/person to Jesus. As you see Jesus take your 'gift', thank him that you can trust him - because he loves you.

Day 4

20 mins   Write down your natural gifts and talents. Imagine yourself laying each of them at the altar before God one by one. Tell God that you voluntarily lay them down and if God never raises them up, then that's all right by you. Tell him that you will use these gifts if he opens up the way for that to happen. Tell him that he means more to you than your gifts. Write down anything that God says to you.

10 mins   Go out for a walk with God. Thank him for who he is and what he means to you. Rejoice that you are in God's family.

Day 5

10 mins   Put on some quiet meditative music without words (perhaps use the tracks from my meditation CDs, 'Smile' or 'Meditations for the Beloved' – you can purchase these from **www.ngm.org.uk/shop**) and read **Revelation 19:11-16**. Use your imagination to see Jesus coming in all his splendour and glory - the King

of Kings and Lord of Lords - the rightful King coming to rule and reign.

Imagine him standing in front of you. Look at his hands and feet. Can you see the nail prints where men cruelly nailed him to a cross? Look at his back and side and see the marks of a wounded man. A man wounded for you and me as he allowed men to hurt him and put him to death on a cross, in order that you and I could have a friendship with our Heavenly Father. Then look into the eyes of Jesus - see the love and compassion he has for you! Hear him tell you that he loves you.

Imagine yourself picking up a crown and putting it on Jesus' head, and as you do, tell him that you love him, and that he is first in your life. Tell him that you want to follow him in every way. Tell him you will go anywhere he tells you to go and you will do anything he tells you to do.

Then imagine Jesus picking up a crown and placing it on your head. Hear him say to you, *"My child, I love you and I am anointing you and I am commissioning you for all that lies ahead. My word to you is to go into all the world and preach the gospel. Let the world see and hear who I am. Let them know that I live."* At the end write down how you felt and anything God said to you.

10 mins   Read and paraphrase **Matthew 28:18-20**.

10 mins   Spend time in worship before the King of Kings.

Thank him for all that he's done on the cross. Thank him for all he's done for you and your family. Thank him for all he's said this morning - then worship and adore him. You might want to put on an appropriate piece of music. (We have a track called 'Blessed Assurance (I Know He's Mine)' on ngm's worship album called 'Assured' – you can find details at **www.ngm.org.uk/shop**) Use body language (kneeling, lying prostrate, bowing, etc., you will find a Biblical list in the Praise and Worship Workout in chapter 2) to express your worship.

Day 6

30 mins   Use a map of your area, or a map of your nation or of the world. Ask God what area/nation he would have you pray for. Write down any area/nation God lays on your heart. Collate (now or within the next few days) any information or statistics you can get about this particular place. Pray and intercede for this area/nation. Pray for the advancement of the gospel, for truth and justice to prevail in the following areas:

1. Leadership (i.e. king; queen; president; ruler; government; local government etc.).
2. The people of the land (e.g. children, old people, one parent families etc.).
3. The Church (use Paul's prayer in **Ephesians 1:16-23**).
4. The media.
5. Education.
6. The business world.
7. Politics.

Spend at least two or three minutes on each subject. Allow God by his Holy Spirit to pray through you. Read **Romans 8:26-27**. Express your weakness to pray as you ought and ask the Holy Spirit to help you intercede. Write down anything God says to you.

Day 7

15 mins   Answer the following questions:
1. **Psalm 37:4** says *'Delight yourself in the Lord and he will give you the desires of your heart.'* What are the desires of your heart?
2. What is your main aim in life?
3. What, if anything, are you doing practically to outwork your main aim?
4. What would you like to see the Lord do in you? Spend time asking God to fulfil that desire.
5. What specifically do you want the Lord to do through you? Write down your answer and ask God to bring it into reality.
6. Spend a few minutes in silence, then ask God if there is anything he wants to say to you. Write down anything he says.

5 mins   Review your memory verse. (**Matthew 5:11-12**)

10 mins   Look through your notes and remind yourself of all God has said to you this week. Thank him for all he's done in you. Ask him to help you to be the person he wants you to be. Commit yourself to him afresh for the future and again tell him you are willing to go anywhere he tells you to go and do anything he tells you to do.

12 Developing a Hunger for God

A question God asked me some time ago was. *'How desperate are you for me to move in your life?'* If we are a desperate people who are hungry for God to move in us, then we will be prepared to pray, fast, live in self-denial or do whatever it takes to get closer with God. One of the stories in the Bible that has frequently encouraged me and I have preached about many times is the story of Bartimaeus. In fact, it has inspired us so much that Ray has co-written a song called 'Shout' about this story.

You can imagine the scene, a man sitting by the roadside begging when, all of a sudden, he hears a commotion - the noise level starts to increase all around him. *"What is happening? What's going on?"* he asks. *"Oh, don't worry,"* he's told, *"It's just Jesus of Nazareth passing by."* His whole being floods with excitement. Jesus of Nazareth! He's the Messiah! If I can just get to him, then my whole life will change. He shouts at the top of his voice, *"Jesus, Son of David, have mercy on me."* Everyone around him tells him to keep quiet. *"Jesus doesn't want to be bothered with the likes of you. Keep the noise down. Just sit there and keep quiet."* Now, at that point, Bartimaeus has a choice. He can sit there and give in to peer pressure, or he can keep going in his desire to get closer to Jesus. What did he do? The Bible tells us that he began to shout even louder, *"Jesus, Son of David, have mercy on me."* Why? The reason was he was desperate to get to Jesus. He knew if he could only get Jesus' attention then his whole life would change.

How desperate are you for God to move in your life? How hungry are you for God? Are you prepared to ignore the other 'voices' that tells us to stay where we are? There are many voices that will discourage us from going deeper with God, some even from friends or family. Yet, if we want God desperately enough we will be prepared to 'shout' with all our might.

Jesus heard Bartimaeus and called him. He asked him, *"What do you want me to do for you?"* It was pretty obvious what Bartimaeus wanted; yet Jesus still asked the question. God knows exactly what your needs are, yet he waits to hear you tell him. Bartimaeus said, *"Lord, I want to see,"* and Jesus replied that his faith had made him well. He got what he wanted.

Another story in the Bible, which is similar to this one, is the story of the woman with the issue of blood. You can read her story in **Luke 8:42-48**. Again she was someone who was desperate to get close to Jesus. Wherever Jesus went, crowds would surround him; however, in this case, the crowd was so vast that it almost crushed him. It was very difficult for this woman to get to Jesus, but she was determined to get close to him, so determined that she probably got down on her hands and knees and pushed through the crowd until she could just touch the edge of his cloak. The ground would have been filled with dirt and filth, because the roads were not cleaned like they are today. Even though it was common for animals to foul the streets, she did not let that put her off. She was prepared to do anything as long as she got to Jesus. She knew that if she could just touch him, then her life would never be the same again. Immediately she touched the edge of his cloak, the power of God went through her and she was totally healed. Again, faith was the ingredient that made her well and she got what she wanted.

Another person in scripture who has inspired me with his determination to go deeper with God is Elisha in **2 Kings 2**. Elijah and Elisha had been good friends for some time. Elisha had served Elijah faithfully and Elijah had been like a 'father in the Lord' to Elisha. Elisha knew Elijah was about to be taken from him, but he wasn't consumed with insecurity, fear or anxiety about the future, because he was consumed with something else. It says that they were on their way from Gilgal, when Elijah says to Elisha, *"Stay here, the Lord has sent me to Bethel."* In other words, *"You stay here, Elisha - this is a wonderful place to be. You will be fine here. After all, this is the 'place of celebration' where the Israelites celebrated the fact that they had put their feet on the promised land. The old had gone and the new was ahead of them. This is a great place to be, Elisha, you stay here, but I'm going on."*

We will always have 'voices' telling us to 'stay here' in our lives. *"Why are you getting so intense about God? Just settle back and be comfortable. It doesn't matter if you don't go deeper with God."* Sometimes, it can be the enemy speaking into our lives, whilst at other times it can be the voice of good and well-meaning friends. Sometimes, however, it can be the voice of God, 'testing' us as to whether we really do want to go on with him. I believe that it was the Lord's voice here that Elisha heard, testing him as to whether he really did want to go on with him. What does Elisha say? *"As surely as the Lord lives and you live, I will not leave you."* So Elijah and Elisha went on to Bethel. The same thing happens here. Elijah says to Elisha, *"Stay here, Elisha. The Lord has sent me to Jericho."* Again, you can imagine Elijah saying, *"This is a good place to be Elisha. Bethel is the 'place of intimacy'. This is the place where Jacob had his dream and he saw angels ascending and descending on a ladder and at the top he saw the Lord. What a place to be, Elisha! Stay here, this is a wonderful place."* What does Elisha say? *"As surely as the Lord lives and as you live, I will not leave you."* So the two of them walk on to Jericho.

Again, at Jericho the same scene happens again. Elijah says, *"Stay here, Elisha. After all, this is the 'place of victory'. This is the place where the Israelites fought and won their first battle. It's an incredible place to be Elisha. Why don't you stay here?"* However, Elisha answers as before. Why was he so determined to go on with Elijah? It was because he was consumed not with insecurity, fear or anxiety at the future, but because he was consumed with having a double portion of Elijah's spirit. In other words, he wanted whatever God had given Elijah. He knew that in order to survive and conquer the future, he needed a double portion of God's Spirit and he was determined to go for it, no matter what the cost. It didn't matter that the road was uncomfortable, long and weary. He was not going to settle back even though these places would have been good places to stop; he knew he wanted more from God.

Elijah asks Elisha the same question that Jesus asked Bartimaeus, *"What do you want me to do for you?"* Again, he got what he wanted. I know it will encourage you to note that the scripture records more miracles happening through Elisha than Elijah. In fact almost double!

What do you want Jesus to do for you? Do you want to go deeper with God? If so, then pursue God with all your strength, and God will give you the desires of your heart

(**Psalm 37:4**). The things that will keep you from pursuing the Lord will be things like tiredness, busyness, lack of appetite for spiritual things, other things like television etc., taking up too much of your time. It's important to remember that in the medical world hunger is a sign of returning health and loss of appetite is a sign of sickness. If you have no hunger for God then you can clearly ask yourself, *"What is wrong spiritually?"* A new hunger is clearly a healthy sign in the church today.

I remember Ray telling me that he spoke to a couple of girls after one of our presentations about going deeper with God. They were telling Ray that they didn't have any hunger for God and wondered if there was something wrong with them. Ray asked if they were Christians and if they had been filled with God's Spirit to which they replied, *"Yes"*. After some discussion Ray felt he should ask them if they spent any time alone with God. They said, *"No"*. They didn't think they needed to spend any time praying, reading the Bible or listening to God. Ray advised them that if they were serious about developing a hunger for God, then they needed to spend time with him soaking up his word. The facts are that his word and his Spirit fuel our hunger for God.

One of the things I constantly pray for myself is that the hunger I have for God and for his word would increase more and more. My prayer for you as you go through this programme is that God would increase your desire for him and for his word and also that through this week God will meet you in a new, fresh and exciting way.

VERSE FOR THE WEEK

'As the deer pants for streams of water, so my soul pants for you, O God'
Psalm 42:1

———

Day 1

5 mins   Write out your aims for this week. Ask yourself this question, *"Do I have a deep hunger in my heart for God?"* Spend a few minutes asking God to increase your hunger for him.

15 mins   Read **Psalm 42**. Ask God to speak to you through this psalm and write down what he says. Also, write down any verses that stand out as you read them.

10 mins   Go for a walk with God and memorise **Matthew 5:6** as you walk.

Day 2

30 mins   Answer the following questions:

1. How much time do you normally spend reading the Bible?
2. How much time do you normally spend in prayer?
3. Do you find reading the Bible hard? If so, why? (I have a Bible planner available which is a

great tool to help you read the Bible – you can order this from **www.ngm.org.uk/shop**.

4. Do you find prayer hard? If so, why?

5. Assess if anything practical could be done to help you if you are struggling with prayer and Bible reading.

6. What is your main priority in life?

7. Assess how much time you spend on the following per week.

a) TV

b) Reading newspapers/magazines

c) Eating

d) Work

e) Leisure outside the home

f) Caring for family members

g) Sleep

h) Church

i) God

j) Any other area

8. Do you feel happy at the way your time is allocated?

9. Pray and ask if God is happy with the way your time is allocated. Write down and implement anything he says.

Day 3

5 mins   Read **Psalm 63:1**. Express to God your need of
          him. If appropriate, tell him that you feel dry
          but that you want to develop a deeper hunger
          for him. Give him permission to do all he wants
          to do in your life.

25 mins   BIBLE STUDY

          Read **Luke 19:1-10**

          1. Zacchaeus had a deep desire to see Jesus.
          He was small in size and because of the crowds
          wouldn't be able to see Jesus clearly. What did
          he do to overcome this difficulty?
          2. Take a few minutes to think and write down
          how Zacchaeus must have felt up that tree (e.g.
          uncomfortable).
          3. Write down how Zacchaeus must have felt
          when Jesus stopped under the tree and spoke
          to him and asked to go to his house.
          4. What happened to Zacchaeus because of
          Jesus' touch on his life?

          Now answer the following questions:

          1. Zacchaeus had a deep desire to see Jesus.
          How desperate are you to have more of Jesus
          revealed to you?
          2. Zacchaeus was prepared to look a
          fool up that tree; he was prepared to be
          uncomfortable. Do you want Jesus desperately
          enough that you are prepared to be pushed out

of your 'comfort zones'?

3. If Jesus was to ask you today, *"What do you want me to do for you?"* What would you say?

4. Spend the remaining time asking God to forgive you for any lack of hunger in your life for him. Ask him to forgive you for any apathy and ask him to fuel a deep hunger and thirst for him and his word. Pray also that God will change you just the way Zacchaeus was changed.

Day 4

10 mins   Read **Psalm 1**. Write down what God says to you through this psalm.

10 mins   Paraphrase **Psalm 1:1-3**.

10 mins   Go for a walk with God. Ask him as you walk to speak to you through what you see e.g. a tree, a river, a building etc. Write down what he says.

Day 5

30 mins   BIBLE STUDY

Read **Genesis 22:1-19**.

1. What was Abraham's relationship like with God?

2. Write down how Abraham must have felt when God asked him to sacrifice his one and only son.

3. Why did God ask him to sacrifice Isaac?

4. Write down what characteristics Abraham portrayed in this chapter.

Now answer the following questions:

1. What is your relationship like with God?
2. If God asked you to give up something or someone special to you - what would you do?
3. Is God first in your life? Is there a relationship in your life that comes before God?
4. Spend an honest time in God's presence. If you can, tell him he's first in your life. Tell him you want to grow in faith, obedience, righteousness and integrity. Ask him to help you draw closer to him.

Day 6

10 mins   Read **John 21:15-19**. Write down what you believe God says to you through this scripture.

10 mins   Meditate on **Matthew 5:6**. Write down what you receive from God through this meditation.

10 mins   Ask God how much he loves you. Write down what he says. Be open to him giving you a vision or picture.

Day 7

25 mins   Read **John 3:16** and **Romans 5:8**. Write them out in full and paraphrase them. Then answer the following questions:

1. Why did God send his Son to die on a cross?
2. What did Jesus give up in order to complete the work his Father gave him to do?
3. Even though we were enemies of God, Christ still came to save us. What does this say to you about God's love and commitment to you?
4. Jesus gave everything for you - if you can, commit yourself to him afresh and thank him again for all his love for you.

5 mins   Spend the remaining time praising God for all you've learned this week. Continue to pray that God would feed your hunger for him and that nothing and no one would come in between you and your walk with him.

13 Seeking God for an Awakening in your Nation

One day in 1985 while Ray was out walking and praying, God spoke to him and said, *"I want you to pray for the nation."* As part of the ministry team Heartbeat, we had been praying and interceding for different parts of the nation for many years but had never prayed for the nation as a whole. We decided that we would start meeting regularly in our home to pray together for the nation. We thought that this was something that would be on the sidelines of our ministry and not necessarily central to our vision which was, 'to be a vehicle for the demonstration of God's power and the reality of his love'. However, after only a few weeks we realised that praying for the nation was going to become central to our vision.

As we had travelled extensively throughout Britain, we were well aware of the state of our nation. Crime was on the increase; abuse, both physical and sexual, of children was rampant. Old ladies were being mugged, raped and sometimes left for dead. The number of people having abortions had increased and a large percentage of teenagers had slept with someone by the time they had reached sixteen. More and more people were becoming homeless and there was much racial tension. We only had to look in our newspapers to discover that our society was in a dreadful mess.

However, it was only when we asked God the following questions: *"How do you see our nation?"* and *"How do you feel about our nation?"* that we broke down and wept. God began to give us pictures and visions about how he saw the nation of Britain.

One of these pictures was of a huge rubbish tip and the smell going up to God was awful. As we prayed, we began to feel God's anger and hurt at a nation turning its back on him again and again. We began to wonder how God could put up with this. Yet, in the midst of all the anger and pain that God felt, we also sensed his incredible love and mercy for our land. We began to repent on behalf of the nation - telling God we were sorry for all the horrible things that went on in our nation.

After a number of weeks of us praying for the nation in this way, God suddenly changed his spotlight, as it were. Instead of shining it on the nation and highlighting Britain, God began to shine his light into our own hearts and lives. What we saw in our hearts under his spotlight broke us again.

We were a ministry team who were on fire for God yet under his spotlight, we began to see things like pride, selfishness, greed in our own hearts and lives that seemed a small reflection of what our nation was like. God even challenged us about saying an unkind word to someone and thinking, *"Well, it doesn't matter - I don't need to put that right."* God was putting his finger on issues in our lives. He said, *"Unkind words do matter! No longer am I prepared to put up with the things that you think don't count."* We began to confess our sins before God and before each other, asking him to forgive us and cleanse us and make us into the people that he wants us to be.

During one of our half-nights of prayer, when there was a real sense of expectancy, God began to speak powerfully through visions and prophetic words. In a vision, I saw an incredibly huge tidal wave, coming in towards the shores of our land. As the wave broke it crashed on to England and spread out to encompass the whole of Britain and went into other nations too. God spoke through this vision and said, *"I am bringing a new wave of my Spirit to this land. Don't look to the old because it will be something new and fresh by my Spirit, and thousands are going to be swept into my Kingdom. I want my people to pray and prepare for all I am about to do, but even if some of my people don't pray or prepare - I am coming anyway."*

What a God we've got! It is not as though we deserve revival, but God in his grace and mercy extends his love towards us. The vision God gave us that evening became central to everything we did. Everything we do now comes out of the conviction that God wants to pour out his Spirit in these last days in a huge and mighty way. We, as the Church, need to be prepared and ready for all he is going to do.

There was a sense in my heart that preparation needed to be inward as well as outward. God wanted his people to purge out anything that was within them that was not of him. He also wanted them to have a BIG vision of what he wanted to do. I was reminded that evening of a scene I saw in Spain a few years earlier, while Ray and I were there on holiday.

We were walking along a street, when we noticed a crowd of people trying to get into a church building. As we drew closer we noticed that the church was absolutely full and that many people couldn't get in. We wondered what was going on, as you don't usually see churches packed to capacity like that. We got as near as we could and peered into the building to discover that it was just a man at the front, preaching. We don't know what he was saying as he was speaking in Spanish; however, God spoke to me very clearly at that moment. I felt him say that the time would come when the churches in Britain would be too small for what he was going to do. There would come a time when churches would be packed and people just wouldn't be able to get in. With all my heart, I said, *"Yes, Lord - do it!"*

As the years went by, God began to plant the word 'revival' on the lips and hearts of people everywhere. I am convinced now more than ever that God is going to pour out his Spirit in a deep way across Britain and many nations of the world. Over the years we have seen God move in incredible ways as he has poured out his refreshment on the Church across the world. However, I believe we still have not seen all that God wants to do.

During our Short-term Teams training in August 1994, as we asked God to come in power, we saw many touched in deep ways. One particular boy was so touched by God, he was staggering around as if he were totally drunk. It reminded me of **Acts 2** when the Spirit of God came on the disciples in the upper room. When people saw them they thought they were drunk with wine. Peter stood up and addressed the crowd and said, *"These men are not drunk, as you suppose. It's only nine in the morning!"* He went on to explain that what they saw was a mighty outpouring of God's Spirit. This boy was behaving as though he had consumed much alcohol but obviously he hadn't. He was totally drunk in the Spirit.

Eventually, when the meeting had finished, we had to carry him to bed and in the morning we asked him what had been happening. He said he remembered worshipping God and then somehow it was as if God took him to Heaven. Jesus spoke to him and said, *"What do you see?"* He said he saw a huge crystal-clear waterfall in Heaven and it was pouring down on the earth. Jesus said to him again, *"What else do you see?"* He said he saw a film covering the earth and this film had some holes in it where some of the water was getting through and sprinkling on the land. Then the Lord said to him, *"The day is coming soon when I will remove the film altogether and the earth will receive the full impact of my Spirit."* What a vision from a fifteen-year-old boy!

Edwin Orr, the great theologian, talks of revival as being something that happens to the Church and a great awakening as something that happens to society. We are beginning to see the first fruits of revival, but our hearts long for much more, resulting in a great awakening right across society. I believe that God not only wants to do so much more with us as the Church, but also wants to pour out his Spirit in such a way that an awakening will happen across the nations of the world. Our hearts respond to him, saying, *"Come, Lord Jesus - do all that's on your heart for this world and pour your Spirit out in deep fresh ways. Let us begin to experience more of your power and grace."*

I do pray as you seek God for a great awakening for your nation that God will pour out his Spirit upon you in new and fresh ways. I know God will use your prayers mightily as you begin to pray and intercede for something that's already on the heart of God.

VERSE FOR THE WEEK

'For the revelation awaits an appointed time: it speaks of the end and will not prove false. Though it linger, wait for it; it will certainly come and will not delay'
Habakkuk 2:3

Day 1

5 mins   Write down your aims for this week. What would you like to see God do in you and through you during this programme?

10 mins   Read **Psalm 36**. Write down what God says to you through this passage. Spend time thanking him for his deep unfailing love for the world.

15 mins   Imagine yourself coming into God's throne-room in Heaven. Ask the following questions about your nation and write down His answers. God will give you pictures, scriptures etc.

1. How do you feel about my nation, Lord?
2. How do you see my nation?
3. Let me see and feel the love you have for my nation.

Day 2

5 mins   Based on the scriptures/pictures you received yesterday - spend five minutes interceding for

your nation.

15 mins   Answer the following questions:

1. Do you have any friends who are not yet Christians? If so - write down their names. If not - think of ways where you could ask God to develop friendships with those outside the Church.
2. Do you regularly pray for them?
3. How often do you pray for your friends at school/college/university/work?
4. Do you know your neighbours? How often do you pray for them?

Ask God to forgive you for times when you have failed to pray for those around you who don't know him yet. Commit yourself to pray regularly for them. Write their names on a piece of paper and put it where you will see it every day. Spend even a couple of minutes at some point during the day praying for them. Ask God whether you should fast for them specifically. Spend time thinking how you could bless them and show them love.

10 mins   Go out for a walk with God. Thank him on your walk for the beauty of the world around you. Thank him for what he means to you and for the friendship you have with him. Bring your friends' names before the Lord and pray for ways to connect with them.

Day 3

10 mins   Go through the following list. All of these things are in your nation. Ask God to reveal if any of the subjects on this list are in your heart and life. Be prepared to allow God who truly sees our hearts to highlight areas that we cannot see.

1. Selfishness
2. Pride
3. Negativity
4. Critical spirit
5. Lacking in love/hardness of heart
6. Bitterness
7. Envy/jealousy
8. Lying (even saying half-truths)
9. Impatience
10. Lacking in kindness
11. Slander (speaking about others behind their backs)
12. Anger
13. Fear
14. Lacking in joy
15. Confusion
16. Rejection (of others, God, self etc)
17. Rebellion
18. Lacking in generosity

Tick those you can see are in your life. God may give you some I haven't mentioned; write them down too.

10 mins   Read **Isaiah 6:1-8**.

            Imagine you opening the door into the Throne
            Room of God and going in to the Holy of
            Holies. See the picture depicted in the first few
            verses above.

            Speak out your repentance at any pride,
            rebellion, etc, that you know is in your life and
            ask God to cleanse you and forgive you. Ask
            God to forgive you for any of the things you
            have ticked above. Acknowledge before God
            that your righteousness comes from Christ and
            from all that he did on the cross for you. Thank
            him for his forgiveness and for his deep love
            for you. Ask God if there is anything he wants
            to say to you and write down what you receive
            from him while you are in his holy presence.

10 mins   Memorise **2 Corinthians 5:17**. Spend time
            thanking God for the encouragement this verse
            brings. Thank God for the newness of life given
            to us through the cross. Ask him to fill you
            with his Holy Spirit.

Day 4

10 mins   Read and meditate on **Philippians 1:3-6**.
            Write down anything God says through this
            meditation.

10 mins   Read **Philippians 1:9**. This is Paul's prayer for the
            Philippians. Pray this prayer for yourself and also
            for the Church in your area and in the nation.

10 mins   Paraphrase **Colossians 2:13-15**.

Day 5

15 mins   Ask God how he feels about the following in
your nation:

1. Child abuse (physical and sexual)
2. Treatment of old people
3. The homeless
4. Abortions
5. Violence (murder, rape, etc)

Spend two or three minutes on each one.
Write down what God says to you.

15 mins   Spend time praying about these five areas and
any more God may add. Allow the Holy Spirit
to intercede with tears, groans, wails etc.,
through you.

After you have finished, thank God that even
though evil is so strong, Jesus is stronger, and
with his help and love we can make a huge
difference in our land.

Day 6

10 mins   Go for a walk with God. Ask God for a picture
of how he sees you. Thank him for his love for
you. Thank God as you walk for his Church
in your nation. Thank him for the army he's
raising up to fight the enemy. Thank him for all
the positive things he's doing at this time.

Read **Ezekiel 37:1-14**

Put on some meditative music (again, my own meditation CDs may help here, you can order these from **www.ngm.org.uk/shop**). Close your eyes and picture the valley that you have just read about. Imagine all the bones lying around - dead, dry bones. Death and destruction lie all around you. Feel the coldness and emptiness of this place.

Now think of situations around you that look impossible or have the touch of death upon them. Perhaps you have been praying for a family member or friend to become a Christian but so far nothing has happened. Perhaps you've been praying for a friend to be healed but again nothing has happened. Whatever it is, I want you to imagine them as those dead and dry bones.

Imagine Jesus standing with you looking at this valley. Hear him ask you the question, *"Can these bones live?"* Respond as Ezekiel did, *"Oh Lord, only you know. This situation seems impossible for me, but I do believe you are the God of the impossible."* Then see the Lord turn and say to you, *"I want you to prophesy to the bones, prophesy to your situations and speak the word of God into them."*

Then speak 'words of life' into them. *"Dry bones, hear the word of the Lord - I speak to you in the name of the living God and I speak the life of God into you."* As you do so, listen for the rattling of the bones as they come together. Look and see the bones and tendons coming together and flesh appearing. See God begin to touch that particular situation.

Then the Lord speaks again. *"Now prophesy to the breath and see the Spirit of God fall upon these people."* As you prophesy the breath and life of God into your situation, begin to see God bring his life to them. Instead of dead, dry bones lying on the valley floor, begin to see a vast, living army. Begin to see your situation come to life in God.

Thank God for his power and love. Thank him for all he's going to do in your situation. Thank him for all you saw as he took you to the valley of dry bones. Pray and intercede for it to become reality in your life.

Day 7

10 mins   Read and meditate on **Luke 10:1**. Write down what God says.

10 mins   Write a psalm to God about your nation and your desires for it.

10 mins   Thank God for all he's said this week. Pray for a greater love in your heart for your nation and for those around you who aren't yet Christians. Pray for a great awakening to flood and drench the land. Use the lyrics of the following song to

pray to God for an awakening for your nation. Thank God for his incredible love for you and your nation. Thank him for all he's doing and all he's going to do.

GREAT AWAKENING

Lord, pour out your Spirit
On all the peoples of the earth.
Let your sons and daughters
Speak your words of prophecy.
Send us dreams and visions
Reveal the secrets of your heart.
Lord, our faith is rising
Let all Heaven sound the coming of your day.

There's gonna be a great awakening
There's gonna be a great revival in our land
There's gonna be a great awakening
And everyone who calls on Jesus they will be saved.

Lord, pour out your Spirit
On all the nations of the world.
Let them see your glory
Let them fall in reverent awe.
Show your mighty power
Shake the heavens and the earth.
Lord, the world is waiting
Let creation see the coming of your day.

Ray Goudie, Dave Bankhead, Steve Bassett.
©1993 Integrity/Hosanna! Music/New Generation Music

14 Developing Positive Waves

Are you always this critical? This was a question a friend asked Ray and myself a number of years ago. We were stunned when our friend Terry, verbalised this question! We had never thought of ourselves as critical. Yet when Terry pointed out that we had criticised a number of musical styles without saying anything positive over a period of a few days, we could see that he was right. With us Brits, it's so easy to criticise rather than encourage or praise. We live in a culture where we look at the negative rather than the positive. In the States or Canada, where incidentally Terry was living, the culture is so different. Everyone seems so positive and friendly.

We are encouraged in the Bible to develop a positive outlook in life and to dwell on whatever is pure, lovely, admirable and praiseworthy (**Phillippians 4:8**), whilst at the same time we are warned to beware of a critical spirit (**Luke 6:37**). Yet, so many of us find it easier to bring others down rather than build them up.

Once, whilst speaking at an event, I happened to give an illustration about a man who used to be a TV evangelist before his whole ministry was discredited. In fact, he was put in prison for many years for fraud. I was emphasising the fact that even in the midst of his trial - when he was at his lowest in prison - as he cried out and asked God *"Do you still love me God?"* God heard him and answered his prayer. The point of the story was to emphasise

God's amazing grace to us all. At the end of my talk a lady anonymously wrote down the following comments, which really saddened my heart. She said she couldn't believe I had used this man as an example as he had hurt so many people. She said, *"he was a greedy man and to deny this undermines the message you gave. I understand he has repented, but he betrayed and hurt many people."*

It quite plainly says in the Bible, *'Do not judge - or you too will be judged. For in the same way you judge others, you will be judged, and with the measure you use, it will be measured to you'* - **Matthew 7:1-2**. It's so easy to be judgmental, totally forgetting that we are all sinners saved by God's amazing grace. The more I go on in this life, the more I realise that I owe everything I have and am to God's amazing grace. If God removed his hand of grace from us and gave us what we deserved, not one of us would be alive today. We all deserve death and hell, yet God in his grace gives us life and the promise of Heaven.

It says in **James 3:5** *'The tongue is a small part of the body yet it makes great boasts.'* Later in **James 3:9-10** it says, 'With the tongue we praise our Lord and Father and with it we curse men, who have been made in God's likeness. Out of the same mouth come praise and cursing. My brothers, this should not be'.

It also says in **James 3:8** that the tongue is a restless evil, full of deadly poison. I don't know about you, but I have often opened my big mouth and said something that I later wished I hadn't. It's so easy to hurt and damage others by careless or insensitive words. One of the decisions I made in my life a number of years ago was to live with short accounts with God. In other words if I said something or did something I later regretted, then I would deal with it quickly rather than ignore it. I would ask God to forgive me, but I would also go to the person or persons concerned and also ask for their forgiveness.

Ray and I were talking just recently about how the negative comments someone has said about you tend to stick in your memory more than the encouraging ones. Somehow negative words have a way of getting underneath our skin. A number of years ago, I served on the UK Evangelists' conference committee and one of the things we did was to ask delegates of the conference to fill in a form giving their comments on how they felt the conference had met their needs. This then gives us a clear idea of how we can serve the conference as a whole. One person who did not put his/her name on the sheet made some very negative personal remarks about me and in particular what I was wearing at the conference! When I read the comments, I tried to think what I could possibly have worn that would have offended someone, but couldn't think of anything that was remotely offensive. At our next committee meeting, the comments were dismissed with a laugh and I was encouraged to ignore it. The committee assured me none of them had noticed me wearing anything offensive, but I did get teased quite a bit, as I am sure you can imagine. It felt good to laugh about it, however, I can tell you those words did sting and the worst bit was that the person had hidden behind an anonymous form thus not giving me any chance to chat to them about it.

It is good to give positive helpful criticism, but it is how we deliver that criticism that is important. We should be like Priscilla and Aquila in **Acts 18**. How they dealt with Apollos was brilliant. Apollos who was a very clever man and a very good communicator arrived at Ephesus and spoke and taught about Jesus accurately. However, as Priscilla and Aquila listened to him preach, they became aware that he did not have the full facts of the message of the gospel. If that had happened in our churches, I wonder if we would have dealt with it in one of the following ways:

1. They could have stood up in the middle of the talk and announced to everyone that Apollos was not preaching the full Gospel. You might think that this would never happen but I have actually seen this take place in the church I went to during the earliest years of my life.
2. They could have taken him aside immediately he finished his talk and told him how he got it wrong. Again, I have seen this happen to quite a number of preachers. This is not a good thing to do because a speaker is at their most vulnerable right after they have delivered their preach.
3. They could have ignored it completely, been really nice to Apollos and not mentioned it to him at all, but behind his back made sure they went round all the congregation and told them to ignore what Apollos had said because he did not preach the full facts of the gospel.

Priscilla and Aquila did not do any of these things, instead, they invited him to their own home and in an atmosphere of love, care and hospitality, they shared with him the way of God more adequately. In other words they made it easy for Apollos to respond well to what they were going to say. They surrounded him with an atmosphere of love and kindness. What a superb example for us to follow. Next time you want to put someone 'right', do remember **Acts 18**.

It's great to know that our tongues can be used to bless and encourage others. So much good can be accomplished by just one word of encouragement. A lady who had been at my 'Spiritual Health' conference in Bristol wrote to me and said, *"Nancy, I thank God for you and your ministry. I want you to know that through it God has changed my life."* When I read her words, my whole being was flooded with encouragement. It was such a blessing to me particularly as the day it arrived I had been feeling very tired and health wise a little below par. Her encouraging words brought tears to my eyes, joy to my spirit and a spring to my step. Reach out in love to those around you. Show them even in small ways the love of Jesus and you'll be amazed at the effect your words can have.

Let's ask God to help us think of good and positive things in life as we train our minds to think on the pure and lovely. Let's embrace positive talk about others rather than harbour a critical spirit, which will in turn leads to bitterness.

———

VERSE FOR THE WEEK
Whatever is true, whatever is noble, whatever is right, whatever is pure, whatever is lovely, whatever is admirable - if anything is excellent or praiseworthy - think about such things.
Philippians 4:8

———

THOUGHT FOR THE WEEK

THINK before you speak

Is it **T**rue
Is it **H**elpful?
Is it **I**nstructive?
Is it **N**ecessary?
Is it **K**ind?

Go through the above checklist before you speak

Day 1

5 mins   Spend time thanking God for your loved ones. Write down their names and thank God for each one. Ask God to bless them in ways they have not yet experienced.

10 mins   Read **Isaiah 53** and spend time thanking God for Jesus. Thank him for all he did for you on the Cross.

15 mins   Read the following meditation called, 'It should have been me'. Imagine yourself to be the person in this mediation.

"It Should Have Been Me!"

In this meditation, I want you to imagine you are a Jew living 2,000 years ago when Israel was conquered by the Romans.

Close your eyes and use your imagination to see yourself in a dungeon. You are a prisoner and you only have a few hours left to live before the authorities are going to crucify you. All sorts of regrets fill your mind - why did I fight? Why did I murder that man? You try to put your thoughts aside - but the anticipation of death ahead seems to cloud and darken your mind. Nothing seems to take away the agony and utter devastation you feel. You joke with the others in your cell that today is your big day - but everything within you is screaming for a way out. You wonder how you are going to face your family and friends. You begin to pray for a brave heart but end up screaming inwardly for God to forgive you and get you out of this mess. Heaven seems to be closed to you and you decide if there really is a God - then either he is sleeping or he doesn't hear prayers from a waster like you. You feel as though your head is going to explode with the heaviness of your thoughts but at that precise moment - the door is opened and your jailer tells you it's time for you to leave.

You get up to walk out of your cell but your legs give way from under you. You stumble across the room knowing that this will be the last walk you will ever take. As you reach the entrance to the cell - you are told you are to be taken to see the governor. You don't understand why - but think this must be one of their 'procedures' before your ultimate journey's end - dying on a rough tree they call a 'cross'. Your heart is beating wildly as you walk into the Governor's room. He takes one look at you and says. *"You are free to go!"* *"Free to go? What do you mean? How can this be? I am due to be crucified today!"* The governor's reply seems to echo throughout the prison, *"You are free because someone else took your place. He was crucified instead of you."*

You can hardly take the words in! Your heart is thumping in your chest - so many questions fill your mind *"Why did someone else die in my place?"* *"Why am I being given the right to live?"* Relief floods through your whole being - you are alive - you are no longer condemned to die - all your guilt has been cancelled out - you are free.

You quickly leave the prison and run outside into the fresh air - you look at the grass, the trees, the leaves, the sky - thankfulness and joy floods your being as you fill your lungs with fresh pure air. On the horizon across the sky - you suddenly see three crosses - you run out of the city to the hill called 'Golgotha' and there in the middle of two thieves is the man who took your place - above his torn and bruised body is the inscription *"Jesus - the king of the Jews"*. You look at his bloodied feet and hands where crude metal has brutally nailed them to the tree. You see his back where it looks as though he's been whipped dozen's of times until his back is like a ploughed field. You look at his head - pierced with thorns until the blood is constantly running down his face. You look into his eyes - and inwardly you gasp because you are surprised at what you see - instead of fear and anger - you see love and forgiveness. He looks straight at you and seems to know who you are. In the depth of his pain he seems to smile and say *"It's okay. It's okay."* You turn away and with tears in your eyes - you shout to the skies *"God - it should have been me! It should have been me! This man has done nothing - it should have been me!"*

© Nancy Goudie

Write a prayer to God thanking him for Jesus and all he accomplished at the cross. Take time to thank Jesus for dying in your place. Rejoice over all that was accomplished at the cross of Calvary.

Day 2

5 mins   Start off today by asking God to forgive you for times when you've been negative or critical. Ask him to show you each time your tongue speaks a negative word.

10 mins   Meditate on **Romans 15:5-6**. Write down what God says through the meditation.

10 mins   Ask God to bring to mind any time you have been critical, negative or perhaps just unkind to someone. Write down the incident and ask God to help you to know how to resolve the issue. If the person knows of your unkind words - perhaps you could write a letter and ask them

to forgive you. Why not send them a little present with a card saying, *"I'm sorry - please forgive me!"*

5 mins   Take time to thank God for the freedom he brings when we begin to put things right.

Day 3

10 mins   In **Romans 13:14** it says, *'Clothe yourself with the Lord Jesus.'* Spend a few minutes meditating on these words and ask God to show you what it means. Write down what you receive from God.

10 mins   Think about a time when someone encouraged you. How did it make you feel? Write down what you experienced through encouragement.

Think of a time when someone was critical, negative or spoke harshly to you. How did it make you feel? Write down what you experienced through negative critical comments.

5 mins   Ask God to help you in every day situations to be full of encouragement. Ask God whom you could encourage today. Write their name on a card or email and then send them a very encouraging note. Make sure that person receives their encouraging word within 24 hours if at all possible.

5 mins   In your imagination and by faith, clothe yourself with the Lord Jesus. 'See' yourself putting on a coat/garment and as you put it on ask God to clothe you with Jesus and drench you with the Holy Spirit.

Day 4

15 mins   Read **Acts 18:24-28**. Ask God to speak to you through these verses and write down what God says. Also write down any practical things you can do to show the same love to others as Priscilla and Aquila showed to Apollos.

15 mins   Meditate on **Hebrews 3:13**. Write down what God says to you through this meditation.

Day 5

15 mins   Look up the following scriptures and write down what they say:

1) **1 John 3:11**
2) **John 15:12**
3) **John 15:17**
4) **Matthew 22:37-39**
5) **Matthew 5:43-45**
6) **Mark 12:28-31**
7) **Luke 6:27-35**
8) **Romans 12:10**
9) **2 John:5-6**

After reading and writing down these verses - ask God to forgive you for not loving others enough and ask him to give you love for the people in your life that you find difficult to love.

15 mins   Ask God to show you if you are holding any unforgiveness against anyone. Write down their name and the reason why. In the Bible it says if we lack forgiveness towards another person, then it hinders God blessing us. You may find it difficult to forgive others especially if they have hurt you badly, but God requires us to speak out our forgiveness even if we don't 'feel' like forgiving them. Withholding your forgiveness will not damage them it will damage you, so take time to ask God to help you with this important task. Then in sheer obedience to God, speak out your forgiveness as you tell God you forgive him/her and at the same time ask him to bring your feelings of forgiveness into being. You may need to do this many times over the coming weeks, months and sometimes even years. However, as you speak out your forgiveness God will change your heart towards those who have hurt you. Thank God for his amazing grace to you.

Day 6

15 mins   Write a love song to Jesus. Express your love for him through writing a psalm of praise. Read it aloud to God.

15 mins   Paraphrase **1 Corinthians 13**

Day 7

10mins   Pray your way through **1 Corinthians 13** e.g. verse **4** says *'Love is patient, love is kind. It does not envy, it does not boast, it is not proud.'* Pray something along the lines of *"Lord help me to show my love for others by being patient - even when I feel like being impatient. Lord, help me to be kind and to show my kindness in practical ways. God forgive me for times when I've been envious, boastful and proud."* Pray like this all the way through this chapter pouring your heart out to God for a deeper knowledge of how to love.

10 mins   Memorise **Hebrews 3:13**. Write it out on cards and place them where you will easily see them. Throughout the day keep repeating the verse to yourself and look out for opportunities to show encouragement to others through your words or actions.

10 mins   Thank God for all the encouragement he gives to you daily. Thank God for others who have encouraged you along life's journey. Perhaps write them a letter thanking them for the input and encouragement they have brought to your life. Ask God to give you a gift of encouragement to pass on to others and therefore bring joy to their lives. Thank God for all you have learned or been reminded of this week.

15 Developing Rhythms of Joy and Peace

Mummy! Daddy! You're home! I remember the days well when, because of our calling, Ray and I would travel away from home sometimes for a few days at a time. It was always such a sacrifice to leave our boys at home as we so enjoy being with them. They are such fun. The nicest bit of going away was always when we walked through the door to experience either Daniel or Aidan running and jumping on us with great excitement and giving us a huge cuddle. Their face always radiated with joy! It was always such a joy to experience such a huge welcome!

Through the years both our boys have brought so much joy and at times we've really needed that joy to take our minds off the stresses and strains that life can sometimes bring. I would say joy is often the emotion that is missing in today's world and especially in the Christian Church. We get so bogged down with our worries and concerns that joy just goes out the window. I remember going out to preach one night feeling really burdened by life's concerns. Before I left, I asked Ray to pray for me. When he had finished he said, *"Just go and enjoy it."* As I reflected on these words I felt the joy of serving God come back. I began to realise afresh what a privilege it is to speak and see God move in so many wonderful ways. Joy began to flood back into my life as I consciously handed my worries and concerns over to God.

A very good friend of mine was telling me recently about

a time when she was rushing for a prayer meeting. Her boys were off school that day and as there was no one to look after them, she took them to church with her. She was already anxious because she was late and on the way there the boys started arguing with one another - the way brothers do. So much so that by the time they arrived at the church it would be a huge understatement to say my friend's nerves were on the edge! She bundled them out of the car and into the creche with instructions to play sensibly and quietly before she joined the others who had already started praying. As she sat down, she noticed that everyone was very quiet and solemn and there seemed to be a heavy atmosphere. My friend is quite an intercessor; she prays regularly for me as I go out to preach and I am always so grateful for her prayers. She is used to storming Heaven and standing in the gap in prayer. In other words, her prayers are not often quiet and certainly are not lacking in energy. She was just sitting there thinking and praying, *"God what this prayer meeting needs is a wake-up call"* when all of a sudden, her boys who were already making quite a noise came rushing into the room blowing a trumpet! She hastily left the prayer meeting, bundled her two boys into the car, highly embarrassed and very annoyed by their behaviour. It was only later that she laughed realising that what she had prayed for happened. The prayer meeting certainly got a very loud 'wake-up' call.

So often we go through life with the heaviest of burdens on our shoulders and yet the Bible tells us that Jesus comes to bring us life and life to the full not life with a small l but life with a capital L.

I remember a time when Ray preached on this particular verse with hilarious results. Ray and I were in Switzerland preaching at various churches and events. As neither of us speak French we always have to use an interpreter. As any preacher or public speaker will know, if you've used an interpreter at any time, the success of your talk depends on how good the interpreter is at translating. The guy we had to interpret was a good friend and someone who speaks excellent English as well as his native language French. So, we anticipated no problems. Ray exhorted us all to live life as Jesus intended. He said, *"Jesus says, I have come to give life and give it to the full. Do you want fullness in your life?"* The audience was silent so Ray said, *"C'mon guys, let me hear you - do you want fullness in your life?"* Everyone again was silent except for me! I thought I'd encourage Ray and show the audience the response Ray wanted. So, I shouted out *"Yes"* very enthusiastically! Ray decided he didn't just want his wife to cheer but he wanted to see the others respond to Jesus. So, he continued to encourage them, *"Let's hear you then - do you want fullness in your life?"* Again I responded with even more energy and excitement, whilst the rest of the audience were completely pan-faced apart from a few people who looked in my direction with a look that told me they thought I was mad! It was at that point that someone from the audience spoke out and said to Ray. *"I think you mean that Jesus said I have come to bring life and bring it to the full - spelt f u l l and not spelt f o o l!"*

The interpreter had got it wrong and instead of Ray saying *"Do you want fullness in your life."* It was actually being translated *"Do you want foolishness in your life?"* No wonder I was getting weird looks as I shouted *"Yes, Yes Yes!"* I certainly felt a proper fool.

We so often forget that God wants us to enjoy life. In **1 Peter 5:7** we are encouraged to 'cast all your cares on to him, for he cares for you'. We often miss out on the fullness of life God has for us, not only because our burdens are so heavy but also because we insist on carrying them ourselves.

Some time ago, I ran a Spiritual Health Weekend conference in Bristol for women called *"Rhythms of Joy"*. My prayer was that when we all left the conference we would 'Go out with joy and be led forth in peace'. One lady told this story right at the end of the conference. She had had a fear of water since she was a very small child. In her youth she had been through a terrifying experience of almost drowning in water. Since that time her fear had taken control. She told us how having met with God in an intimate way during the conference, God had released her from this fear. She was seen swimming several lengths in the swimming pool much to the amazement of her friends. She certainly went out with joy and was led forth in peace.

I've discovered that the only way to deal with the stresses and strains of life is to sit at the feet of the Lord Jesus. Even though at times your circumstances can feel so dark, God's joy can always penetrate through. I remember waking up in the middle of the night some time ago and even though it was so dark outside I could hear the birds singing! God spoke straight into my heart at that precise moment and said, *"Nancy always remember that when you think circumstances around you are very dark, take your example from the birds and start singing. As you praise me, you will begin to realise that dawn is only around the corner."* Often God encourages us to praise him despite our circumstances. Remember Paul and Silas in their Philippian jail in **Acts 16**. They had been badly beaten and thrown into jail, yet the only crime they had committed was the fact they were

Christians. Right in the middle of their torment, right in the middle of their dark night, they began to praise God. Instead of being bitter, resentful and angry at God and at their circumstances, they were filled with joy and began to sing. Can you have joy in the middle of stress? The answer is Yes. I mentioned earlier that just recently my husband went into hospital for a major life threatening operation. Just before going into the operating theatre, he was filled with such joy, peace and even an excitement as he sat in God's presence. Sit in God's presence and know his deep and wonderful love for you. No matter how dark your circumstances are, you can start to sing again. My prayer this week is that in the midst of your busy, stressful life that God will meet with you so much that it has you jumping up and down in sheer excitement and pure joy.

————

VERSE FOR THE WEEK

'You will go out in joy and be led forth in peace;
the mountain and the hills will burst into song before you,
and all the trees of the field will clap their hands.'
Isaiah 55:12

————

Day 1

5 mins   Read **Psalm 20**. Thank God that he does bring joy and peace into our busy lives and especially at times when we are feeling laden down with cares and worries. Ask him to start a work in you that will lead you to experience greater freedom in the areas of joy and peace.

15 mins   Write down any cares, stresses or worries that you have at this time. After compiling your list, go through each one with God in prayer. As you pray about each one, see yourself in your imagination, handing them over to God. Afterwards, thank him for taking your cares but make sure your leave each one in his strong arms.

10 mins   Memorise **Isaiah 55:12** and claim this verse for yourself. Say it to yourself every day this week and ask God to make it real for you.

Day 2

30 mins   BIBLE STUDY

Read the book of Philippians. As you do underline and count how many times Paul uses the words joy or rejoice.

Answer the following questions:

1. Where did Paul write this book? See **Philippians 1:12-26**.
2. How would you have felt if you, like Paul, had been put in prison for a crime you did not commit?
3. Does joy appear in your answer to the above question? Write down any reasons you can think of that would enable Paul to talk about, write about and feel joy.
4. Spend time asking God to help you to see above your circumstances and not sink below them.

5. Spend the rest of your time this morning praising God. Use your body as well as your words to praise him and release your joy.

Day 3

10 mins   Meditate on **Isaiah 43:2**. Write down what you receive from God.

10 mins   Go out a walk with God. Ask him to show you things in the street, park or wherever you are walking that brings joy to his heart.

10 mins   Think and write down any way you can bring joy to God's heart this week. Make sure you do them before the week is over.

Think of and write down ways you can bring joy to others you meet from day to day. Again, make sure you carry them out before the week is over. Often bringing joy to others will release joy to us.

Day 4

5 mins   Start today with a song of joy. Read **Isaiah 12:1-2** out loud to God and verses **3-6** to yourself.

10 mins   Paraphrase **Isaiah 43:1-2**. Write a prayer of thanks to God and speak it out loud to him.

10 mins   Meditate on a piece of chocolate (or your favourite kind of food). Use all your senses in

this meditation. Look at the chocolate, feel it, smell it, taste it and ask God to speak to you through it. Write down what you receive from God.

5 mins   Thank God for the joy he brings and continue to speak out **Isaiah 55:12**.

Day 5

10 mins   Write a psalm of joy to God. When finished, read it aloud to him. I know it will really bless his heart to hear your psalm.

10 mins   Memorise **1 Thessalonians 5:16-18**. Ask God to speak to you through these verses. Write down what you receive from God.

10 mins   Read **James 1:2-4**. Reflect on how you feel when you face a trial or problem in your life. Do you respond with joy? If you are being honest the answer is probably *"no"*. Ask God to help you through any trial or difficulty you may experience in the future and to know his deep joy even in the midst of problems.

Day 6

10 mins   Read **Psalm 126**. Write down what God says to you through the reading of this psalm

15 mins   Go for a walk with God. Tell him how much you love him. Ask him to fill your heart with joy. During your walk again ask God to show you

ways you can share your joy with others. Write down what God says and make sure you do what he says as soon as possible.

5 mins   Speak out **Isaiah 55:12** again and continue to claim this verse not only for yourself but for others too.

Day 7

5 mins   Revise your memory verses for this week. Speak them out in prayer.

10 mins   Think of any friends or family who are currently going through tough times. Write down their names and bring them to God one by one. Write down anything you receive from God for them. Write them a card letting them know what encouragement God gave you for them. Make sure you give it to them as soon as possible.

10 mins   Read **Matthew 5:1-12**. Ask God to speak to you through this passage. Write down what God says.

5 mins   Thank God for all he has taught you about true joy this week. Ask him to help you to experience his deep joy even through the deepest sorrows. Finish this week by speaking out **Isaiah 55:12**.

16   Knowing You Are Special

"Nancy, I can't book into your Spiritual Health Weekend," said a friend in an email to me. When I asked her why, her answer totally surprised me! She said, *"It's because of the title of your weekend, 'You are Special'. I am not special and I will never be special."* How sad and yet I wonder how many of us have maybe believed this at some time in our lives? The truth is that every one of us is very special. Each human being is a unique and remarkable individual. We are all different and yet each one of us is so special. There is no one quite like you. Yet many people think, *"I am unique - I am ugly and stupid like no-one else!"* Sometimes we just cannot see ourselves as someone who is extra special.

When I was a child, I remember quite vividly being told by someone who was annoyed with me that no one would ever want to be my friend. Isn't it funny how the negative things you hear seem to stay with you much longer than all the encouraging comments? Although I knew that the person who had said those words loved me and didn't mean them, the impact of them remained with me and at certain times haunted me. When I met and married the most wonderful likeable guy, at times I used to think that people only liked us because of Ray rather than because of both of us. It was only when a close friend of ours told me that she loved being my friend that it seemed to release me from the lie that had been sown all those years ago. I have met many who believed the lies that others or even life itself had sown into them.

Ray and I have met many girls and guys who hurt

themselves because of the pain of negative words. Others have developed eating disorders often because of careless words spoken by others. We met a girl whose mother constantly spoke hurtful and negative words about her; eventually that beautiful girl believed the lies and thought she was ugly. She started to cut herself as this seemed to be the only way she could deal with the pain. This girl and many like her believed the lies that had been spoken about them. They didn't realise that they were special, that they were unique and wonderful, but through the years it has been incredible to see that as they began to believe the truth about themselves, it set them free to be who God had created them to be,

I remember a time when my husband told me, *"I'm glad I'm me! I don't want to be anyone else but me. I don't want to be Billy Graham. I don't want to be Andrew Lloyd Webber. I love being me and I'm glad God made me, me!"* I wonder how many people reading this book can say the same? Are you glad God made you the way you are? So many of us wish we were someone else. There's a story I used to tell to children years ago called Camelephantelopelicanary! It's a story of a Camel who didn't like the way he looked and as he looked around him, he often wished he looked more like the other animals he saw. One day as he was walking through the jungle he saw an elephant and immediately said, *"Oh, I wish I could look like an elephant. If I had a trunk like an elephant then I wouldn't need to stoop for my water. I could use my amazing trunk and then I would be really happy. Oh, I wish I had a trunk like an elephant."* As quick as a flash, he suddenly had the trunk of an elephant.

He then thought to himself, *"I really need to change my name because I am not just a camel anymore, I'm really more like a camelephant.* So he called himself Camelephant. Camelephant was very happy with the way he looked until he happened to see an antelope. He saw how fast an antelope could run and thought to himself, *"Oh, I wish I had the legs of an antelope."* As quick as a flash, he suddenly had the legs of an antelope. He could not believe it! He was extremely happy and thought to himself, *"I'm not really a Camelephant any longer, really I am more like a Camelephantelope."*

Camelephantelope was very happy as he walked in the jungle. He thought he had everything he wanted until he happened to spy a pelican. He saw how a pelican was able to store his food in his beak and before he could stop himself he said, *"Oh, if only I had the beak of a pelican then I would really be happy! Oh, I wish I had the beak of a pelican."* Again, as quick as a flash he had the beak of a pelican. So he said to himself, *"I'm not a Camelephantelope any longer, my name should be Camelephantelopelican."*

Caelephantelopelican was now extremely happy! He was very pleased with himself and life seemed very good until he heard a glorious voice. It was a canary. This bird had an amazing voice and once more he opened his mouth and said, *"Oh, if only I had the voice of a canary! I so wish I could sing like that! Oh, I wish I had the voice of a canary."* As quick as a flash, he then had the voice of a canary! He thought to himself, *"I'm no longer a Camelephantelopelican any more. My name should be Camelephantelopelicanary!"*

Camelephantelopelicanary was really pleased with himself. He thought life could not get any better.

Around that time there was a meeting of all the animals

in the jungle. The lions were there, the tigers were there, in fact every animal in the jungle came to this important meeting and so Camelephantelopelicanary went to the meeting too. When he walked in, everyone stopped and stared at him. Then someone laughed, and soon everyone was in fits of laughter. They were all laughing and pointing at Camelephantelopelicanary!

Camelephantelopelicanary was devasted. He suddenly saw himself in a mirror and realised how strange he looked and before he could stop himself he groaned and said, *"Oh, I wish I was just a camel again!"* As quick as a flash he became a Camel again.

The moral of this story is that we always want to look like someone else. We want what they have – a cute nose, great skin, beautiful hair, but we forget just how amazing each one of us is. Each one of us is special. Each one has been created in the image of God. Each one has qualities that are wonderful and amazing. Let's remember that we have been created by love and fashioned by grace and that there is no one in this world who is more wonderful than you!

In my book 'You Are Special', I explain what the word 'special' means. I have written, *'Special applies to something or someone who is admired, precious, unique and cannot ever be replaced. Special best describes – YOU!'* As you go through this programme, my prayer is that you will find out that you are someone who is admired, precious, unique and indeed very special.

More on the subject of being special can be found in my book called 'You are Special' – visit **www.ngm.org.uk/shop** to order.

―――

VERSE FOR THE WEEK

My lover spoke and said to me, "Arise, my darling, my beautiful one, and come with me.
Song of Songs 2:10

―――

Day 1

5 mins   Ask God to reveal to you this week just how special and incredible you are! Take time to lay down your preconceptions about who you are and tell God that you are eager to listen to his voice this week as he tells you how special you are!

15 mins   Read **Genesis 1:27** – *So God created mankind in his own image, in the image of God he created him; male and female he created them!*

Meditate on this verse and write down what God says to you through this verse. Each day this week take 2 minutes to remember that you have been created in the image of God. You are a person of worth and value!

10 mins   In my book, 'You Are Special', there is a list of 7 reasons why you are special:

You were chosen before the creation of the world.
You are loved completely and unconditionally

You are unique, one of a kind. There is no one exactly like you.
You were given a precious gift – the gift of LIFE.
You were fashioned in the womb by kind and loving hands.
Someone gave his life so that you might live.
You are never forsaken not forgotten.

Take time to read each of these reasons out loud to yourself. You may want to add more reasons why you are special. Speaking these reasons over yourself will help you to really know that you are indeed a wonderful and special human being.

Day 2

15 mins   If you have my meditation CD 'Peace Like A River', then play Track 1 called 'You are Special'. This exercise obviously works best if you have the CD, but if you do not have it, then you can read the words here.

After you have read the words or listened to the track, then write down what God has said to you through this meditation.

You are Special

Believing you are special is difficult for most of us. We often need reminding that there is no-one quite like us. If you are anything like me, it will be easy to think negative thoughts about yourself, and perhaps even about your body;

wishing you were different, more likeable, more shapely. I want to take you on a journey, that will help you see that you have been sculpted and formed by kind, gentle and loving hands, and that in all the world there is no-one quite like you.

Take a couple of deep breaths, breathing in through your nose and out through your mouth. Then speak to your soul, and say: *'Listen soul, to the voice of truth.'* Now close your eyes and come with me on a journey of truth.

Now begin to use your imagination to see in your mind a man sitting in a workshop, working with a piece of clay. You look at the clay, and you wonder if he could make any beautiful thing from something that looks so ugly. You watch as he gently, but firmly moulds the clay, and as you do, you realise this is a master craftsman at work. You watch his large hands craft the most delicate of pots, each detail is completed with expert skill. It does not seem to matter how long this creation takes to make, as long as when he is finished, he rejoices in it. You notice that as each lump of clay gradually disappears, what takes shape before your eyes is an amazing sculpture. He lovingly shapes his creation; he takes time over fine details, to make sure everything is perfect.

You realise that this potter does not make any mistakes, he does not make something and then discard it, but he rejoices in what he is making and is delighted with each of his creations. Each one is different, and yet so special. As you watch, listen to the voice of truth within you. Truth speaks to you and says, *'Just as this potter moulded and crafted this piece of clay, so did I mould you in your mother's womb. You are not a mistake, but gentle, loving hands created you. Just as each of this potter's creations are special, so are you special.'*

As you begin to leave your meditation, say to yourself several times, *'I am Special. There is no-one like me. I was shaped, formed and crafted in my mother's womb. I am wonderfully made. What a creation!'*

Any time you feel ugly, unloved or negative about yourself, remember the potter. Go to a mirror, and repeat the words, *'I am special, there is no-one like me.'* Train yourself to say these words many times, because unless you are able to love and accept yourself, you cannot fully love others

© Nancy Goudie. Meditation on Peace Like A River CD

5mins   Take time to pray and thank God for the way he sees you and for the way in which he values you.

10 mins   Go for a walk. Remember, as you look at the birds in the sky that **Luke 12:6-7** says this: *"Are not five sparrows sold for two pennies? Yet not one of them is forgotten by God. Indeed the very hairs of your head are all numbered. Don't be afraid; you are worth more than many sparrows."*

Thank God as you walk that he loves you and values you!

Day 3

10 mins   Mediate on **Ephesians 1:4**. Write down what you receive from the Lord. Also write down how it makes you feel to be called and chosen before the foundation of the world was put in place.

20 mins   Read **Psalm 8:4** which says, *What is mankind that you are mindful of them, human beings that you care for them?* Ask God this question and write down what he says to you!

Look up **John 3:16** and write down what it says in relation to your question above.

A friend is defined by being someone who knows everything about you and still totally accepts you as you are.

Look up **John 15:15** and write down what it says.

Look up **John 15:16** and thank God for what it says.

Read **Romans 5:6-8** and write down how it makes you feel.

Spend time thanking God that he deeply loves you and regards you as his friend.

Day 4

30 mins   Sometimes in life we can feel overlooked or forgotten, but God will never forget us! Look up **Isaiah 49:15** and do the following:

Meditate on this verse and write down what you get through your meditation.

Paraphrase this verse by putting it into your own words.

Memorise this verse and confess it frequently throughout today.

Spend the remaining time thanking God that you are never forgotten.

Day 5

20 mins   Read page 17 of my book called 'You Are Special'. If you don't have a copy of this book then this is what it says.

I'm Glad I'm Me!

One day as my husband and I were chatting, he said to me, *"I'm glad I'm me. I don't want to be Billy Graham. I don't want to be Andrew Llyodd Webber. I don't want to be anyone else but me. I love being me! I love the creativity that God has given me and I'm glad God made me, me!"*

There are many who cannot say what my husband said that day! There are many who eagerly desire to be someone else. We look at others around us and wish we had been born with their beauty, creativity, talent, gifting, finance, etc. We think their life must be so much better than ours. What we have missed is the beauty we have within and how much our life is worth. What we have missed is how much we are valued and loved. Each one of us has been chosen and each one wonderfully made. God looks at you now and says, *"You are beautiful from head to toe; absolutely flawless!"* (**Songs of Songs 4:7**) God wraps his love around you and clothes you with his joy. You are special, a joy to behold. When you begin to believe these truths, then you can say with enormous truth and conviction, *"I'm glad I'm me!"*

Write down any reasons why you cannot say, *"I'm glad I'm me!"* Analyse why you have these reasons in your life. Lay these reasons down before God and ask him to change your mindset with his truth.

Then begin to thank him, even if you don't feel it, that you are you! Thank him that he sees you as a special and unique human being. Thank him that he loves you and has called and chosen you.

10 mins   Memorise **Matthew 6:26** and keep repeating this verse to yourself for the rest of the week.

Day 6

10 mins	Write a psalm of praise to God thanking him that he has made you unique and special and thanking him that he loves you so very much. Read your psalm out loud to God.
20 mins	Read **Luke 15** – The story of the Prodigal Son.
	Write down what this story tells you of the love of the father.
	Examine the way the father loves both of his sons.
	Look at how he yearns every day for the return of his son. He looks for him every day expecting to see him in the distance.
	Write down all that you can learn from this story about Papa God's love for you.
	Finish by writing a prayer to God thanking him for his unconditional love and acceptance of you.

Day 7

5 mins	Revise your memory verse for this week. Speak it out in prayer.
10 mins	Think of a way you can tell a friend that he/ she is special. You might want to write them a card, buy them a book, give them a CD,

something to let them know that they are a unique, precious and wonderful human being. Make sure you write your card etc. soon and give it to your friend. Everyone needs to know they are special.

10 mins   Read page 57 of my book called 'You Are Special' which is called, 'Do you Know?' If you don't have the book, then this is what it says:

Do You Know?

Do you know you are more precious than silver and more valuable that gold? Do you know that I created you in the secret place and formed you in the womb; that I crafted you with love and moulded you with grace? Do you know I chose you to be mine before the world was created? Do you know I made plans for you, plans to prosper you and not to harm you, plans to give you hope and a future?

Do you know?

Do you know that from the beginning I have lovingly carried you in my arms? Do you know that my loving gaze is upon you and that my fragrance is poured over you? Do you know that every day I place my kiss upon your soul and I hug you to myself? Do you know that I have willingly given all for you and I would do it all again!

Do you know? Do you know?

Ask God to make these truths real in your life. Revise these truths many times throughout your life.

5 mins   Hopefully you have been remembering every day to thank God that you are made in his image and that you are a person of worth and value. If you have not remembered to do this then take some time right now to do so. Then spend some time thanking God for all he has taught you about yourself this week. Thank him that you are a wonderful and very special human being and that he loves with an unconditional love.

Finish by looking in a mirror and speaking the words 'you are special' over yourself.

17   Dance the Dance of Love

As I mentioned before, I became a Christian when I was six years of age, but although I knew at that age that God loved me, it was many years later that I discovered that God had loved me before the foundation of the world was put in place. He loved me even before I was born and every day he lavishes his love upon me. This wonderful truth is the same for you too. No matter who you are God loves you. Whether you are black, white or coloured, whether you are rich or poor, large or small, old or young, gay or straight, a Christian or not a Christian, God still loves you! Jesus said in **John 3:16** that God loves the world. He didn't say that God loves only certain people; he said God loves the world and that includes you and me! Wow! This gospel is such good news! It's not bad news, its brilliant news! Jesus said he had come into the world to bring life and life to the full. Knowing the love of a kind, loving, happy God brings us life in all its fullness.

When my husband Ray and I were in our early years of marriage, I remember Ray asking me the same question again and again. *"How do you know, really know that God loves you?"* I struggled to give Ray an answer that would satisfy him. I told him that I just knew that God loved me. I had an inner conviction in my heart that I was loved, as well as many scriptures that confirmed what I was feeling. Ray knew the scripture but he didn't have the conviction in his heart. He had struggled in the early part of his life with pornography and that had left him with guilt and shame. Even though he had forgiven himself for what he had done, it must have left a mark upon his life. One day God spoke to Ray and asked him to come up close and personal with him. Ray went into his study, sat down with his pen and journal ready to hear from God. He was ready to write down the vision he assumed that God wanted to share with him. Instead God gently whispered into his ear these life-transforming words. *"Ray, you are my beloved son in whom I am well pleased."* The words broke him and he cried and cried. He then knew for the first time that God really did love him despite his past.

When you know you are loved it changes everything. I wonder if you know, really know that God loves you? When you do it frees you to be the person God created you to be

I tell a story in my 'Beloved' book about two brothers. They could not be more different. The older one had everything! He was clever, confident, was blessed with good looks, had loads of friends and had everything going for him. The younger brother was not clever, or good-looking, in fact he had a hunchback and very few friends. He was not confident; however he had an amazing singing voice. He used to fill the house with songs of joy.

When the brothers were at boarding school, the older brother did not want anyone to know that the boy with the hunchback was his younger brother. One day the brother with the wonderful voice was picked on by some boys at his school. They called him names and ripped off his shirt to expose his deformed back. The older brother who was an admired leader of the student body knew what was happening, but chose not to intervene. The younger brother felt betrayed by his brother by what he failed to do. He left the school and from that day on he never sang again.

Years passed and the subject of that day was never spoken about. One day the other brother realized what he had done. He was full of remorse and travelled hundreds of miles to come home and beg his brother's forgiveness. The two brothers talked long into the night and they hugged and cried together as forgiveness flowed. During the night, the older brother awoke to the sound of beautiful singing, which flooded the house. His younger brother was singing again.

When we know we are loved, it frees us to be the person God created us to be. Do you know you are loved? God calls each of us to know and to experience the depths of his love for us.

The Bible says that God is love. To experience real true love you need to know the depth of love that exists in the Trinity. The Father loves the Son and the Son loves the Holy Spirit and the Holy Spirit loves the Father and therefore there is this circle of love between the Godhead. The early church fathers explained it in this way: If you have ever been to a Greek wedding, you will have seen their distinctive way of dancing. It's called perichoresis (a dance), which is apparently where we get the English word choreography from. In the Greek dance there are not only two dancers but there are at least three. They start to go in circles, weaving in and out in a very beautiful pattern of motion. They start to go faster and faster whilst at the same time staying in perfect rhythm and also in sync with each other. Eventually they are dancing so quickly that as you look at them it just becomes a blur. Their individual identities are part of a larger dance. The early church fathers and mothers looked at the Greek dance (perichoresis) and said, *"That is what the Trinity looks like."*

It's a harmonious set of relationships in which the Father loves the Son, the Son loves the Holy Spirit and the Holy Spirit loves the Father. It's a circle of love. All three are loving and serving each other. This is the dance of God, the dance of love.

The great news is that we are included in this dance of love. We are already in! As I said at the beginning of this chapter we are called and chosen from before the world began. God has already included us, but often we just don't realize what God has done for us. We stand outside looking in, instead of joining in on the dance of love and experiencing love and life in all its fullness. God has given us a place in the amazing circle of love, joy, freedom and peace that the 'three in one' enjoy. He has made a way for us, but often we have settled for second best. CS Lewis said this, *"Indeed if we consider the unblushing promises of reward and the staggering nature of the rewards promised in the Gospels, it would seem that our Lord finds our desires, not too strong, but too weak. We are half-hearted creatures, fooling around with drink, sex and ambition when infinite joy is offered us, like an ignorant child who wants to go on making mud pies in a slum because he cannot imagine what is meant by the offer of a holiday at the sea. We are too easily pleased"*

Let's not settle for second best when we could join in on the dance of love and discover freedom and joy like never before. Let's experience acceptance, intimacy, security, let's totally live life to the full in the inheritance that is ours in Christ. Come on, let's trust him and ask him to fill us with new wine and hear our Papa tell us that we are his beloved child in whom he is well pleased!

VERSE FOR THE WEEK

How great is the love the Father has lavished on us
that we should be called children of God!
And that is what we are!
1 John 3:1a

Day 1

5 mins   Ask God to reveal to you this week the way
he lavishes his love upon you every day. Ask
him to show you through a vision, picture or
through a verse in the Bible how he has loved
you even before you were born.

10 mins   In my book called 'The Beloved' I tell this story
called 'The Kiss of God'.

I had just seen the amazing film, 'The Passion
of the Christ'. Many parts of the film had made
a deep impression on me, but particularly the
place where Jesus kisses his mum. It was the
only lighthearted bit in the film where Jesus
was making a table and there was a bit of jovial
talk between them both. Suddenly, he leans
over and kisses his mother on the cheek. My
reaction was 'Wow, I wish Jesus would kiss me
like that!'

The next morning as I thought through what I
had seen the night before, in prayer I turned to

the Lord and said, *"I would really love it Lord if you would kiss me like that"*. Immediately the answer came back. *"Nancy, I kiss you like that every morning!"* I was stunned! Then the tears began to flow as I realized afresh how much my God loves me! My Jesus had kissed me like that every morning of my life and I had not realised it.

© Nancy Goudie

The truth is that the Lord kisses each of us like this every day. Today, thank the Lord for his kisses and ask him to make you more aware of his love and gentle kisses every day.

15 mins   The disciple John called himself 'The Beloved'. John was someone who knew he was loved extravagantly. Spend a few minutes asking God to reveal his extravagant love to you and pray that you can show this amazing love to those around you every day.

Read **1 John** and write down every verse in this book where John mentions the word love.

Once you have written each verse then go through each of them and write down what you can learn about love from these verses.

Finish by thanking him for his extravagant love for you and ask him to show you ways of showing that incredible love to others today.

Day 2

10 mins   Memorise **1 John 3:1a**.

How great is the love the Father has lavished
on us, that we should be called children of God!
And that is what we are!

15 mins   My husband has written a song called 'Dance
of Love'. Here are the lyrics. Take time to read
through them and ask God to speak to you
through them. Write down what the Lord says.
Write down anything that comes to mind as
you read these lyrics:

Grace sweeps like a wild storm
Into the corners of our shame filled mind
Like refreshing rain turned into wine
We drink and leave the past behind
Past behind

Surrounded by the Trinity
We dance the dance of love
The gift of life, such ecstasy
We dance the dance of love
Accepted in the family
Now we are the beloved

We dance the dance
We dance the dance
We dance the dance of love

We dance the dance of love
We dance the dance of love

We dance the dance of love
We dance the dance of love

Grace falls like a meteor
Exploding love on our fear filled hearts
Like a burning heat that melts the chains
And moulds a brand new work of art
Work of art

Grace like lightning in the sky
Lights up the truth and strikes the lies
Hear the sound of thunder in the night
Echoing love through our lives
through our lives

Lyrics by Ray Goudie © New Generation Music 2015.

5 mins   Go through your memory verse again and
write it down so that you can take it with
you wherever you go. During the week keep
revising your memory verse.

Finish by thanking the Lord for including you
in the dance of love. Remember to dance with
the Trinity today wherever you go.

Day 3

10 mins   Read **John 3:16** in the Amplified Bible:

For God so greatly loved and dearly prized the
world that he [even] gave up his only begotten
(unique) Son, so that whoever believes in
(trusts in, clings to, relies on) him shall not

perish (come to destruction, be lost) but have eternal (everlasting) life.

Write a prayer to God telling him how you feel when you read that he greatly loves and dearly prizes you. When you are finished – read it out aloud to the Lord.

20 mins   BIBLE STUDY

Read **2 Samuel 11** then answer the following questions:

Write down all the things that David did wrong in this chapter.

What could he have done to avoid all these things happening?

What does this teach you about your own life?

What does it say in the last verse about how the Lord viewed what David had done wrong.

Read **Acts 13:22**. Even though David was a murderer, an adulterer and a liar, God still called him 'a man after my own heart'. What does this tell you about our God?
1 Samuel 16:7 says God looks at the heart rather than the outward appearance. How do we keep our hearts pure (see **Psalm 119:9**)?
Read **Psalm 139:23-24**. This is a psalm of David. Finish by giving God permission to search your heart and see if there is anything

there that needs dealt with. If there is, then take time to bring your confession before God and ask for his forgiveness knowing that when he has forgiven, it is forgotten. Thank God for cleansing your heart today.

Day 4

15mins   Read **1 Chronicles 17:16-18** then make this prayer of David's personal to you.

Say to the Lord, *"Who am I O Lord God and what is my family that you have brought me this far? And as if this were not enough in your sight O God you have spoken about the future of the house of your servant. You have looked on me as though I were the most exalted of men/ women, O Lord God. What more can I say to you for honouring your servant? For you know your servant."*

Now take time to listen to the Lord and write down what he says to you.

10 mins   Spend time worshipping the Lord. You can use a track on the New Generation Worship EP 'Assured' called Blessed Assurance (I Know He's Mine). Allow the words of the bridge to go deep into your spirit.

And I believe I am his child
I know I'm loved forever
I can hear his song of hope
He sings 'you're my pleasure'

Joy and peace fill me each day
His life is now my treasure
I am his I know he's mine
I know he's mine

Lyrics by Ray Goudie © New Generation Music 2015.

5 mins   Review your memory verse for this week and at
the same time thank God for his great love for
you.

Day 5

10 mins   Meditate on **Psalm 52:8** - *But I am like an olive
tree flourishing in the house of God; I trust in
God's unfailing love for ever and ever.* Write
down what the Lord says to you through this
meditation.

15 mins   Write down as many adjectives as you can
which describe the love of God e.g. Unfailing
love – **Psalm 52:8** and find a verse that has this
description in it. You may want to use Bible
Gateway or a concordance.

5 mins   Go through each word that describes God's
love and thank him that the truth is that his
love is unfailing etc.

Day 6

10 mins   Paraphrase **1 John 3:1a**. *How great is the love
the Father has lavished on us that we should be
called children of God! And that is what we are!*

10 mins   You belong to God and to his family. Write
           down how the words 'belonging to God' makes
           you feel. Write down any problems you may
           have when you consider this truth. Write down
           the good things you feel when you consider
           this truth.

10 mins   Go for a walk and thank God as you walk that
           no matter what happens you belong to him.
           You belong in the wonderful amazing dance
           of God. No one else can take your place. God
           has lavishly poured out his love in our hearts
           (**Romans 5:5**). Thank him that he takes our
           guilt and shame. Take time on your walk to
           thank him for this fact.

Day 7

10 mins   There are so many psalms where David talks
           about his love for God. Write your own psalm
           telling God how much you love him.

10 mins   Go through **Psalm 23** and write down each
           thing God does for us.

10 mins   **1 Peter 5:7** tells us that God cares for each of
           us. Take time to thank him that he cares so
           much for you. Keep reviewing your memory
           verse and thank God for all the love he lavishes
           on you every day. Thank him for all he has done
           this week. Ask him to continue to open your
           eyes to the depth of his unfailing, unconditional
           love for you his wonderful child.

18 Discovering the Gift of Laughter

I heard a story recently about a Catholic school run by nuns that really made me laugh. As the children were queuing to get their lunch they noticed a bowl of apples with a sign on it saying, *'Take one apple only – God is watching you!'* Further along the line, there were a plate of chocolate chip cookies and one of the children had written a note on it saying, *'Take as many as you want, God is watching the apples!'*

Laughter is an amazing gift given to us by God. There are so many benefits of laughter. Laughter can relax us, lift our mood, help us lose weight and even smooth our wrinkles! What a gift! Did you know that one good belly laugh burns off 3 to 4 calories? Were you aware that laughing only 15 seconds can add two days to your life span? The truth is laughter can improve our health in so many different ways. Laughter massages the heart as well as other vital organs in our bodies and can prevent heart disease and heart attacks. Stress is one of the biggest contributors to high blood pressure and laughter is a brilliant antidote to stress. Studies have shown that only ten minutes of laughter can reduce blood pressure. It is also true that when we laugh it can make us feel as though we have been on an instant vacation! That's why so many people go to hear comedians these days! Laughter makes us feel so good!

Experts tell us that laughing for 15 minutes can give us the same benefit as two hours of sleep! People have discovered that a diet of reading funny stories and watching comedy films can have a significant effect on your physical health. Many patients have been told to watch funny films, read books that will provoke laughter and keep company with people who make them laugh for this has sometimes restored their health. Laughter is good for you physically, mentally, emotionally and spiritually. It's a great medicine that has incredible healing powers and the good news is that it is free. It doesn't cost a penny, but the best news of all is that it has no side effects! Since Ray went through an operation to remove a cancerous tumour in his pancreas, we have discovered how every drug he takes has side effects and some of these side effects can cause him to be quite ill. To know that God has given us an amazing gift which has healing powers and yet no side effects is so wonderful.

Often however, we forget what a beautiful and very helpful gift God has given us. Did you know that we were all born with the gift of laughter? It's a wonderful free gift from God to each of us. Have you ever watched a baby laugh? They laugh so easily and at almost anything. No one has to teach a child to laugh – it happens naturally. The statistics tell us that this is true. Did you know that on average a child laughs 300 times a day, whereas an adult laughs on average only 4 times a day!! What happened to all our joy? We have forgotten that we possess the gift of laughter! As we grow older worry, fear and anxiety steal our joy away until we lose the ability to laugh in difficult circumstances.

I read recently about a nurse who had compiled a list of the top five regrets people have when they have come to the very end of their lives. Among them was, *"I wish I had let myself be happier."* At the end of life, no one had a regret that they wished they had experienced more sex, work, or exciting bungee jumps, but one regret many had was that they hadn't laughed more. The nurse recorded, *"Many did not realise until the end that happiness was a choice."* Let's not forget to learn from the children around us and laugh often! Let's make sure we give ourselves permission to laugh!

When Jesus was here on earth he said that he came to give us 'life to the full'; I cannot imagine life to the full without having fun, laughter and joy. Can you? Jesus spoke so much about joy and encouraged those around him to rejoice even in difficult circumstances. But can we do this when we are going through tough times? Jesus encouraged his followers to follow the pathway of joy even when facing problems and difficulties. It says in **Hebrews 12:2** that when he faced the barbaric death of dying on a cross, it was because of the joy before him that he endured the pain and the suffering. His joy was knowing that everyone could now experience a joy filled life!

There is obviously a time to laugh and a time to weep, a time to dance and a time to mourn, as it says in **Ecclesiastes 3:4**. All these emotions are right and appropriate at various times throughout our lives, but let's not discard joy and laughter for it is these gifts that will help us all get through the tough times of life.

When my husband went through a 12-hour life threatening operation earlier this year to remove a cancerous tumour in his pancreas, it wasn't a time where much laughter resounded. Yet even in the midst of tears, problems, heartache and difficulties, there were times where I laughed. For a number of weeks a dear friend in ngm called

Ruth took me into the hospital when I didn't trust myself to drive. She has a great gift of humour and so every day as I shared with her some of the funnier stories that happened to Ray whilst he was recovering, she and I laughed together in the car. Those times were so therapeutic for me. The laughter helped to release some of the stress and lifted my spirit. Laughter is such an amazing gift from God. The experts tell us that a good hearty laugh will relieve stress and tension and will leave our bodies relaxed up to 45 minutes! So look for opportunities to laugh no matter what you are going through; it's a tranquilizer with no side effects. As an Old Irish proverb says, *A good laugh and a long sleep are the best cures in a doctor's book.*

My prayer is that through this week you will discover a pathway of joy and laughter that will help you through even the most horrendous times of life – it certainly did for me!

———

VERSE FOR THE WEEK
I have told you this so that my joy may be in you, and your joy may be complete.
John 15:11

———

Day One

5 mins   Thank God for the gifts of joy and laughter and ask him to reveal to you this week how these gifts can help you in your everyday life.

10 mins   Paraphrase the verse of the week, **John 15:11** knowing that this verse was said by Jesus when he was here on earth. Write down what you have learned from paraphrasing this verse.

10 mins   Meditate on **Acts 2:28** - write down what you get from your meditation.

5 mins   Read **Psalm 16:11** – this is where **Acts 2:28** is taken from – but it has an extra line – *with eternal pleasures at your right hand*. This verse states that there are eternal pleasures at the right hand of God. Write down what God says to you through reading this verse.

Day Two

25 mins   Often laughter is the missing ingredient in people's lives and yet God wants to bring laughter to every one of us. Abraham and Sarah discovered this for themselves.

Read **Genesis 21:1-7**. Answer the following questions:

God gave Abraham and Sarah a promise – what was it? See **Genesis 12:7**; **Genesis 13:14-17**; **Genesis 15:4-5**; **Genesis 17:15-16**; **Genesis**

17:19-21; **Genesis 18:10**. Write these verses out in full.

2. Why was it such an amazing miracle when Sarah became pregnant? What does this say to you about believing God for the impossible?
3. How long did it take for Abraham and Sarah to receive God's promise? What can you learn from this?
4. Verse **6** tells us that God brought laughter to come to live in Abraham and Sarah's house. How did he do this?
5. Verse **6** says that everyone who hears Abraham and Sarah's story will laugh with them. What can you learn from this?
6. Abraham and Sarah tried to work out the promise of God but despite what they did, God brought his word into being. What does this teach you about the heart and love of God?

5 mins   In the remaining time, go a short walk with God and ask him to bring laughter to live in your home (heart).

Day Three

15 mins   Read **Proverbs 31:10-31**. These verses talk about a wife of noble character. Now read verse **25** and in particular the words – *She can laugh at the days to come.*

Read **2 Corinthians 7:4**

Read **2 Corinthians 8:2**

Write out what each of these verses say about
the circumstances of joy and laughter and write
down what this tells you.

10 mins   Answer the following questions:

Analyse how often you laugh in any 24 hours.
Write down places or events where laughter
seems to happen naturally – why is this?
How do you feel when you do laugh?
What stops you from laughing?
How can you increase laughter in your life?

Fear and worry are often the joy stealers – Find
a verse in the Bible that tells you what to do
about worry and then find one about fear.

5 mins   Thank God for the gift of laughter and for
the joy he has given us and tell him you are
choosing joy and laughter over worry and fear.

Day Four

10 mins   Write out **John 15:11** several times and then
memorise this verse. Write it down on a card
so that you can take it with you and revise it
throughout today.

15 mins   Meditate on **Job 8:21**. Write down what you
receive through your meditation.

5 mins   Think of ways of how you can encourage
yourself and others to laugh naturally. Put this
into practice in your life.

Day Five

15 mins   When you go through tough times, it can
be difficult to smile, never mind find joy and
laughter. Yet even smiling in the storm can
help us discover peace through the hard times
of life. Find a place where you can listen to my
Meditaton CD entitled 'Smile'. Use track 4 of
my Meditation CD called 'Smile'. This exercise
works better if you have the CD, but if you
don't have it, then read the following words of
the meditation. When you are finished, write
down what you felt God say to you through this
meditation.

Smile

Laughing through a storm or smiling in the rain
can often be difficult for most of us. However,
when the storms of life surround us or the
winds of change overwhelm us we can indeed
learn to laugh and to smile at what the future
holds.

Are you going through tough or overwhelming
times? Are you discovering that life is too
difficult and the pain too great? Then take a
deep breath, slowly breathing in and slowly
breathing out as we look at how we can change
our feelings and change our world.

Now close your eyes, focus on your feelings and
begin to smile. This may seem unnatural for
you at the beginning, but even if you don't feel

like smiling, try it anyhow. Make up your mind to choose to smile. Don't stop smiling until the music fades and by the time the music is finished my prayer is you will begin to feel your joy return.

As you keep on smiling, turn your attention to all the good things that have happened in your life. If you look for them, there will be many. It may be a kind deed someone did for you, it may be a job you got or a gift you were given. It may be a good friend, the health you have or even the clothes you wear. Look for them and list them in your mind and begin to say thank you for each one as you continue to smile.

Now, I want you to remember a beautiful memory, a funny moment, a future event you are looking forward to, or someone who has brought you lots of love and laughs. Focus on this, but if at any time you find your mind wandering back to the pain and you feel the rain of the storm returning, then keep turning your mind to something pure, lovely, positive and admirable, something that is excellent and worthy of your praise and at the same time keep smiling. If you continue to think good and positive thoughts then the summer sun will begin to shine upon you.

Begin to come out of your meditation, but don't stop smiling. Your circumstances may still be the same, the future may still look bleak, the road ahead may still seem hard, but as we smile and change our feelings we can find peace even in the middle of a storm. Each time you find life difficult, dwell on the positives, look for the things you can be grateful for and remember - smile!

© Nancy Goudie

10 mins   Read the words of Jesus in **Luke 6:21**, *Blessed are you who weep now, for you will laugh.* Stand in front of a mirror and repeat this promise to yourself many times. Then spend time thanking God for his promise whilst reminding yourself that what God promises he fulfills. (See **2 Corinthians 1:20** and **Joshua 23:14**)

5 mins   Read and meditate on these words from **1 Peter 5:11** (The Message) and thank God for his great plans for you! *This suffering won't last forever. It won't be long before this generous God who has great plans for us in Christ -eternal and glorious plans they are - will have you put together and on your feet for good. He gets the last word; yes, he does.*

Day Six

20 mins Read **Genesis 1:27**. This verse tells us that whether we are male or female, black, white or coloured that we have all been created in the image of God. If we have been made in the image of God then it is obvious that the God who has created us to enjoy the gift of laughter will laugh too. However, many people find that concept hard to accept. It doesn't seem to match up with their picture of God. Answer the following questions:

What picture do you have in your mind of God? Is he a happy God? If not, why not?

Read **Psalm 2:4** and you will discover that God laughs. Write down any reasons you have as to why you find it hard to imagine God laughing. Look up the following verses and write down what Jesus said he would give us in each of these verses.

John 10:10
John 3:16
John 17:13
John 16:33
John 16:13
John 20:22

When you read these verses what kind of picture does this give you of God?

10 mins   Write a prayer to God thanking him for who he
           is and for all he has given you.

Day Seven

5 mins   Review your memory verse.

15 mins   Write a psalm to God thanking him for joy and
           laughter. Once you have written it – read it
           aloud to God.

10 mins   Write a list of any changes you would want to
           make after discovering this week that you have
           been given the gift of laughter. Decide how to
           make yourself accountable for these changes
           and put this into place in your life.

Spending Time in the Garden with God

'When are you going to come and see me then, Nancy?' This was a question a very good friend of mine had asked me again and again over a number of years. Unfortunately, because of our schedule and family commitments, we don't often get to see our special friends as much as we would like. Every time Ali, my friend, asked me to visit her - my heart said, *"Oh yes I want to very much indeed"*, but my schedule said, *"No way."* She had come over to see me at my home quite a number of times over the years but since the arrival of my second son, it had become difficult for me to find extra time in my busy schedule to visit her in her home in Northern Ireland. However, I did promise her that I would come and see her. You see, even though I am busy, I want to visit her and spend some special time with her, but the only way that is going to happen is if I look at my diary and put it in as a priority. So that is what I did. It can be the same when it comes to God. When God calls to us, *"Come and spend some time with me"* our heart may say, *"Oh yes Lord I'd love that"*, but because of the busyness of our day often our special time with God can be squashed into a small place rather than having the priority it deserves. Again, similar to me visiting my friend, we need to look at our schedule and see when we can have that special time in God's presence. On top of our special daily time with God, Ray and I sometimes mark out a special day or days when we will spend time praying and seeking God. Our complete leadership team at ngm go away together usually about two or three times a year to pray and seek God together.

Those times we spend away with God are very special and we often come back feeling that they are just too short. It's all about relationship; it's not a duty or trying to win brownie points! He is with us 24/7 but we all need those intimate times where we are just hanging out with God in his beautiful garden listening, laughing, just being with him and enjoying his company.

In the Bible Jesus encouraged his disciples to *come apart and rest awhile.* He knew the strains and stresses of everyday ministry meant that the disciples needed to spend quality time alone with him. He also knew that he needed to spend time with his heavenly Father and at several times *'got up early when it was still dark* and was completely alone with God.

In the Old Testament, God encouraged Elijah after a very hectic and stressful time, to come away with him to receive fresh vision and instructions from him. This time for Elijah was mega important and gave him clear vision for the future as well as God encouraging him and building up his confidence in God.

The enemy knows how important it is to spend quality time with God and therefore will try to discourage you from doing so at every turn, and even when you have decided to spend a day or a portion of the day in prayer, he tries to distract you with one hundred and one different things filling your mind. When people I met started mentioning that to me, I started to write Spiritual Health Plans for them so that they could follow a programme right throughout their day. The difference was amazing. I received letters and comments from people telling me how God had spoken to them as they had prayed and sometimes fasted too. Many said that the day seemed to pass so quickly, but at the same time they received so much from God. I would encourage you to put aside quality time with God, where God can speak straight into your situation. I know you will come back refreshed and blessed. I have written a number of day programmes that you can use when you spend a day or a period of time away with God. If you wish to fast during this time, make sure you have read the instructions in this book about fasting and have prepared for it.

Every year at the beginning of the year, I run two conferences, one in Bristol and one in Preston. It's a weekend where you will not only experience fun and laughter, but you will also go deep with God and experience him in ways that will change your life. It's a time for women of all ages to come away and spend an intimate time with God in the relaxing environment of a four-star luxury hotel. Without the usual pressures of work, home or family life, it is easier for people to go deeper with God than they have ever gone before. Here's a couple of the letters I received.

"Dear Nancy,

I wanted to write and thank you for leading such a wonderful weekend in Bristol. I didn't really have a chance to speak with you, but I want you to know that Jesus has blessed me so much. I feel changed - a different person to the worn out Mum who arrived on the Friday evening!

The weekend enabled me to renew an intimate relationship with God that I had not felt since before I had children (8 years!) The sessions you led on hearing God through the objects, chocolate, flowers etc., and listening to hear him give Bible verses for other people, encouraged me so much. God showed me something each time, so my faith soared. This week, I have been using your book, Spiritual Health Plan, and have found it excellent in helping me go on in the areas I grew at the weekend - thank you.

I also fasted for a day (a thing I have found very hard in the past) and had an excellent time and saw my family really affected. In many ways, it is with my children day in, day out that I've noticed God has changed me. He has given me patience, more love and understanding and they are different because of what Jesus did in me at the weekend.

During the communion service at the weekend, God healed me physically. I have had bad tennis elbow for three months and it is completely gone now. He also reminded me of all kinds of injuries and illnesses I have had over the years since I was small, and I felt he was healing all the past hurts and pain and putting it behind me so that I was ready to enter into the exciting future ahead.

Once again I want to say a huge thank you to you and your team for an absolutely brilliant weekend. I feel like a new woman."

JN - Kent

"Dear Nancy,

First may I say a very big thank you to you and all your team who were ministering in the name of Jesus at the 'Rhythms of Joy' conference. I thank my Father God for you all and pray that he will bless you abundantly.

I am 61 years of age and have had many problems over the years. The last four years of my life have been like walking through a minefield. However, the Lord has been with me through it all and I have received great support from my home church and my brothers and sisters in the Lord. At the end of November last year, there was a verse in my quiet time readings, which came like a promise from God. 'The God of grace will soon crush Satan under your feet'. The following week there was a notice on the church sheet saying that a group of our younger ladies were coming to your Spiritual Health Weekend and they invited us to join them. My prayer partners had been suggesting for a while that I needed to get away and spend time with God, but it had not been possible because of family needs, but it was clear to me that I had to come to this weekend - so I booked in. Praise the Lord, he knew my needs and because of you and your team, I received so much healing and renewing, both physically and spiritually. I sat in the Jacuzzi and as I'm only just over 4.7 tall, my feet did not touch the floor. I floated on top of the bubbles as they came up and it felt so wonderful. I felt God was saying, "I will hold you safe in everything."

Then during the sessions, I received so much from God. I was able to let go of so much baggage, so much frustration, so much fear and leave it all at the cross of Jesus. As I surrendered myself to the Lord, the blessing was immense and the encouragement tremendous. What I have put on paper is so little of what this weekend has done for me. One of the young ladies in your team said she saw me as a giant woman of God - well, I really feel I am walking tall today and will continue to do so as I walk with my hand firmly clasping that of my Lord and Saviour Jesus Christ. God bless you all."

MS - Warwickshire

If you want to find out more details of my Spiritual Health Weekends, then look online at **www.nancygoudie.com**. Or you can write to me at ngm, Caedmon Complex, Bristol Road, Thornbury, Bristol, BS35 3JA and I will send you the information.

Can I encourage you to look at your diary now and put time aside when you can perhaps do one of the following day programmes and have a quality time with God. You will find that after you have spent time with your Heavenly Dad you will no longer be the same person. I know God will impact your life and the lives of the people for whom you are praying. Go for it!

Daily Workout Programmes

1. DISCOVERING H.O.T. FAITH

9.00 - 9.15   Write your aims for this day spent in the presence of God. Then spend some time asking God to begin to fulfil these aims today.

9.15-9.45   Read **Hebrews 11**. Write down what God says to you about faith through this chapter.

9.45-11.15   Bible Study 1.

11.15-11.30   Drink and rest.

11.30 -12.00   Go for a walk. Memorise **2 Corinthians 5:7** as you walk.

12.00-12.30   There are three steps to developing H.O.T. Faith – Hearing, Obeying and Trusting. The first is hearing - answer the following questions:

    Read **Romans 10:17** – what does this tell you about faith?
In what ways can we hear from God – write each one down.
How easy/hard do you find it to hear from God? Give reasons for your answer.

What ways do you normally hear God speak to you?
What would stop you from hearing from God and what can you do about this?
What do you find easy or difficult about faith?

12.30-1.45   Drink and rest.

1.30-1.45   The second step to developing HOT Faith is obeying. Read and meditate **1 Samuel 15:22** and **James 1:22**. Write down what God says to you through meditating on each of these verses. Write down what you learnt about obedience? What can you do to make sure you respond to God with obedience?

1.45-3.15   Bible Study 2.

3.15 - 3.30   Drink and rest.

3.30 - 4.00   Read **Matthew 15:21-28** taking particular notice of the words of Jesus in verse **28**.

Jesus said to the woman *"Great is your faith"*, because despite the circumstances that surrounded her – she did not give up! Even when she is met with silence, receives a negative reply and eventually gets told that she is asking for the wrong thing, she doesn't give up! What an amazing thing to hear that Jesus says her faith is great.

Then read **Luke 8: 22-25** and again notice the words of Jesus in verse **25**

These words were spoken to the disciples who had seen Jesus heal everyone who came to him. They had seen the deaf hear, the dumb speak, the blind see, and even the dead being raised yet when it came to their own storm, Jesus had to ask them, *"Where is your faith?"*

When you are going through a storm, take note of what this woman did and don't give up! Find another story in the Bible where the person did not give up and was rewarded for their tenacity. Then spend time asking God to forgive you for the times when you have 'given up' and make up your mind that even if your faith fails, you will still get back up on your feet again and keep walking the walk of faith.

4.00 – 4.30   The third step to H.O.T. Faith is trust.

Read **Joshua 3:7-17**. The Lord told Joshua to tell the priests to go and stand in the river even though the river was in flood at that time. It looked as though it was impossible to cross this river. Look at the story and write down everything that would have been hard for Joshua, the priests and the people to do to trust in God during this time.

Verse **16** tells us that God began to do a miracle when the priests heard, obeyed and started to trust God. God did the miracle out of their sight at a town called Adam. It was only as they stood where God told them to stand that the water would gradually go down and eventually the river would disappear. What does this teach us about trusting in God?

4.30-4.45   Paraphrase **Matthew 17:20** and then meditate on this verse and write down what you receive from God through your mediation.

4.45-5.00   Review your memory verse. Write down what you have learned during today about faith. Go for a walk and thank God for the faith you do have and ask him to increase your faith in the days, weeks, months and years to come. Tell him you want to hear him say to you, *"Great is your faith!"*

BIBLE STUDY 1

1 Kings 17: 1 – 9

Read these verses at least twice and then answer the following questions:

This is the first story in **1 Kings** about the prophet Elijah. As you read these verses what kind of a man is Elijah?

Elijah did something really significant in Verse **1**. He went to the King of the country and told him what the Lord had said. That is the equivalent of going to 10 Downing Street and telling the Prime Minister that there will be no more rain in this country until you say so. Write down what this verse tells you about Elijah and also what it says about his relationship with God.

God backs up Elijah's word and there is no rain in the land. How long does this last for? See **James 5:17**

God understands that Elijah needs his help to stay alive when the whole country is going through a drought and so he tells him what to do. He hears the word of the Lord telling him what to do. Write down as many ways as possible in which you can hear the word of the Lord.

The Lord told Elijah to hide in the Kerith Ravine and that he would provide supernaturally for him there. Write down any way you or any of your friends or family have seen God provide supernaturally.

When Elijah hears the word of the Lord, he immediately obeyed what God has told him to do. How hard/easy do you find obeying what God tells you to do. What would stop you from obeying God?

When Elijah obeyed God, he then trusted that God would do what he said he would do. How hard/easy do you find trusting God and why?

Elijah found that God was faithful for quite some time, but then he began to notice that the brook that the Lord had said would provide water for him was drying up. What kind of thoughts might have gone through Elijah's mind?

He was seeing before his eyes the end of his provision. Write down what thoughts Elijah might have found difficult. Can you identify with this?

Every day the brook got less and less, yet Elijah did not move from the place God had told him to go to. What does this teach you about waiting on God and staying where God put you until God speaks again?

It was only when the last of the provision had gone, that God spoke to Elijah again and told him what to do. He was on the verge of a new adventure, but he could not start the new adventure until the present adventure had finished. His faith in God grew through hearing, obeying and trusting God right to the end. Write down what this teaches you about faith?

Write down anything that would stop you from hearing, obeying and trusting in God? Then write down ways to overcome each difficulty.

BIBLE STUDY 2

Read 1 Kings 18: 41-46

Read these verses twice.

Elijah had told the nation that there would be no more rain in the land until he says so – see **1 King 17:1**. We are going to look at what he did when the time came for the drought to stop.

Elijah told the King in verse **41** that there was a sound of heavy rain in the land – yet the skies were still blue and the earth was still parched. How do we know that Elijah was not speaking out of presumption? Look at Chapter **18:1** for the answer. What does this teach you about faith?

While Ahab ate and drank – what does Elijah do? See verse **42**. What does this teach you about faith?

While Elijah prayed he kept asking his servant to go and look toward the sea. Why did he do this?

When his servant came back saying he could see nothing – in other words Elijah had not yet seen the answer to his prayers of faith – what did he do? What does this tell you about a journey of faith?

Elijah refused to give up even though there was no sign of God working but he choose to believe the words he had heard from God that rain would come on the land. Think of the challenges you face right now and write a prayer to God - first of all ask him to speak into these challenges and then tell him you will work them into being by being obedient and by trusting him.

Elijah in verse **44** gets told that there is a cloud the size of a man's hand. In the natural this is not enough to bring loads of rain, but Elijah has heard from God and has obeyed God (Chapter **18:1-2a**) and now he trusts God that what God has said he will do. The small sign is there and now he tells his servant to go and tell the King to go back to his palace before the rain stops him. What can you learn from this?

It was only after Elijah had completed this journey of faith that the skies grew black (verse **45**), a wind rose and a heavy rain came on. What does this teach you about walking the walk of faith in your everyday life?

Spend some time asking God to increase your faith and help you to hear, obey and trust. Elijah had an amazing faith, yet in **James 5:17** it tells us that Elijah was just a man like us. In other words he was not any different to the rest of us – we can have a faith like this too if we have intimacy with God and hear, obey and trust him.

2. DEVELOPING TRUST IN GOD AND OTHERS

9.00 - 9.30   Read **Psalm 37:1-6**. Write out these verses in full. Underline the verses that speak to you the most. Spend time praying about what God says to you through these verses.

9.30 -11.00   Bible Study 1.

11.00-11.15   Drink and rest.

11.15-11.45   Go for a walk. Memorise **Philippians 4:13** as you walk.

11.45-12.30   Read **Proverbs 3:1-10** three times.

1. Paraphrase the whole section
2. Memorise verses **5** and **6**
3. What is trust? Define the meaning.
(Use dictionary, concordance etc.)
4. What areas of trust do you find difficult?
5. Do you find it easy/hard to trust God? and why?
6. Do you find it easy/hard to trust others? and why?
7. Write down each blessing God promises through this portion of scripture.
8. Spend the remaining time praying. Ask God to increase your level of trust in him and in others.

12.30-1.30   Drink and rest.

1.30-3.00   Bible Study 2.

3.00-3.15   Drink and rest.

3.15-3.45   Read **Isaiah 25:9**. Thank God for his
                  faithfulness. Spend time praising God
                  for all his faithfulness to you. Use biblical
                  ways of expressing your praise i.e. singing,
                  clapping, dancing, shouting, kneeling,
                  raising hands etc. Try expressing your
                  praise to God in ways you haven't used
                  before. It might be helpful to use a
                  worship album.

3.45 - 4.30   There are many instructions in the Bible
                  exhorting us to 'trust God'. There are
                  many benefits from doing so. Look up
                  each scripture reference and see what God
                  promises. Write out the verses in full.

                  Psalm 22:4-5
                  Psalm 25:2-3
                  Psalm 32:10
                  Psalm 37:3
                  Psalm 37:5-6
                  Psalm 40:4
                  Psalm 56: 3-4
                  Proverbs 3:5-6

We are told in the Bible what we shouldn't put our trust in. Look up each of the following scripture references to discover what we should not trust. Write out the following verses in full.

Psalm 44:6
Psalm 49:5-7
Psalm 146:3
Jeremiah 17:5
Jeremiah 48:7

Read **Jeremiah 17:7-8**. Meditate on these verses and write down what God says to you through it.

4.30 - 5.00   Spend some time repenting of the times when you have failed to trust God or others. Acknowledge your failure - then commit yourself to God. Imagine yourself on a road with God. Where you would like to be in the area of trust may seem many miles down the road, but all that God requires of you now is to take the first step. Put your hand into his and walk with him. He'll be there to help you. (Taking a step forward with him means trusting him in situations you find difficult.)

BIBLE STUDY 1

2 Corinthians 1

Read the chapter at least three times.

1. Who wrote **2 Corinthians**?
2. When was it written?
3. Where was it written?
4. To whom was it written?
5. What is he trying to communicate through this chapter?
6. Meditate on verses **3** and **4**. Write down what God says to you.
7. If you have been hurt or damaged in your life, then read verse **5** again. What does it mean to have God's comfort in our lives? Has this happened to you? If not, why not?
8. Paraphrase verses **5**, **6** and **7**.
9. According to verse **9**, why did Paul and his companions go through such trials and sufferings?
10. What does verse **10** teach us about Paul's trust in God? Could you trust God in similar circumstances?

BIBLE STUDY 2

2 Corinthians 2

Read the chapter at least three times.

1. How can we stand firm in our walk with Christ?
2. How important is faith to God? Find a verse in scripture that tells you.
3. What is Paul trying to communicate through this chapter?
4. How should we deal with a repentant sinner?
5. How important is it to forgive sinners? See **Mark 11:25**
6. How easy/hard do you find it to forgive those who have hurt you? and why?
7. Meditate on verses **14** and **15**. Write down what God says to you.
8. Paraphrase verses **14** to **17**
9. Verse **15** says we are the aroma of Christ. What does this mean?
10. What does it mean to 'peddle the word of God for profit'?
11. What verse/verses speak to you the most and why?

3. HOW TO DEAL WITH DOUBTS

9.00 -9.15   Write down any specific aims you may have in spending this time with God and ask him to begin to fulfil them in you today.

9.15-9.45   Read **Psalm 46**. Write down what God says to you through this chapter. Spend time praising God for who he is and for all he does for you.

9.45-11.15   Bible Study.

11.15-11.30   Drink and rest.

11.30 -12.00   Go for a walk. Memorise **John 14:1** as you walk.

12.00-12.30   Answer the following questions:
1. How did you become a Christian?
2. How easy/hard do you find talking to God? Give reasons for your answer,
3. How easy/hard do you find listening to God? Give your reasons for your answer.
4. How do you cope when you receive bad news?
5. Do you tend to be a pessimist or an optimist? How does your answer affect your walk with God?
6. What is faith and how do we exercise faith practically? Find a verse in the Bible that tells you what faith is.

12.30-1.45   Drink and rest.

1.30-1.45	Read and meditate on **Romans 10:9-11**. Write down what you get.
1.45-2.15	Look up the following references. Write down what happens when people believe and do not doubt.

Mark 5
Mark 9:20-25
Matthew 21:18-22
Matthew 8:5-13
John 11:17-44
1 Peter 2:6

Speak out your faith and trust in God to fulfil all His promises. Look up **1 Thessalonians 5:24**. Write out the verse in full. Paraphrase the verse. Spend time praising God for his faithfulness.

2.15 - 2.45	Write down the meaning of the word 'doubt' as found in the dictionary.

Read **John 20:24-31**.
1. How does Jesus deal with doubt?
2. What is his promise to us who believe yet have not seen?
3. Write down the areas where you find it difficult to trust and easy to doubt.
4. Try and assess why you find it difficult to trust in these areas.
5. What does the Bible say about someone who doubts? Look at **James 1:6-7**.

6. Ask God's forgiveness for your lack of faith and ask him to increase your faith

2.45-3.00   Drink and rest.

3.00-3.30   Go for a walk. Thank God as you walk for who he is and what he's done for you.

3.30-4.00   Look up **Philippians 4:13** and **Hebrews 13:5b**. Write down the things you find difficult in your Christian life. Go through each one with God, speaking out these verses into each situation. Spend five minutes allowing God to speak to you. Write down what he says. Ask God to fill you with his Holy Spirit and declare your faith and trust in him.

4.00-4.30   Write down all the good things God has done in your life. Spend time praising God for all he's done for you. Express your worship using the whole of your body - i.e. use dancing, singing, clapping, shouting etc. Tell God how much you love him.

4.30-5.00   Go through all your notes. Write down what you have learnt or what God has done throughout today. Thank God for all he has accomplished.

BIBLE STUDY

Acts 3-4:31

Read the passage at least three times.

1. Who wrote the book of Acts?
2. When was it written?
3. To whom was it written? and why?
4. Compare Peter and John's behaviour in these two chapters to how they behaved in **Mark 14:43-72** and **John 20:19**. What was the difference? What had made them so bold?
5. Peter and John use every opportunity to share the good news about Jesus with the crowds. How do you feel about sharing your faith with others? and why?
6. Spend time asking God to forgive you for missed opportunities that come to mind and ask God to enable you to speak with great boldness. See **Acts 4:29**.
7. The consequence of Peter and John's witness and preaching on this occasion and others was being thrown into prison. What was their response to this? See **Acts 5:41-42**.
8. We may not be persecuted in this way, but we may 'suffer' in other ways, e.g. be laughed at, scorned, made to look a fool, ignored etc. How do you cope with these things?
9. Why did the high priest and Sadducees have problems with the beggar being healed?
10. Memorise **Acts 4:12**.
11. Read **Acts 4:13**. Write down what the Lord says to you through this verse.
12. **Acts 4:11** and **25-26** quote Old Testament scripture. Where can you find these verses in the Old Testament?

4. HOW TO DEAL WITH WORRY AND STRESS

9.00-9.30   Read **Psalm 146**. Write down what God says to you through this psalm and spend time in prayer and praise thereafter.

9.30-11.00   Bible Study 1.

11.00-11.15   Drink and rest.

11.15-11.45   Go for a walk. Meditate on and memorise **Philippians 4:6** as you walk.

11.45-12.30   Read **Luke 10:38-42**. Answer the following questions:

               1. Why was Martha so upset, annoyed and worried?
               2. Why did Jesus say that Mary chose the better way?
               3. Can you identify with Martha?
               4. Write down what you can learn from this story?

               Read **Luke 12:22-31**. Answer the following questions:

               1. List all the things that Jesus tells us not to worry about.
               2. Do you find yourself worrying about similar things? If so, spend some time asking God to forgive you for worry and concern and ask him to give you his peace.

3. Read verse **24**. Do you consider yourself valuable to God? If not, why not?
4. How do we 'practically' seek his Kingdom?

Spend the remaining time praying to God about your answers.

12.30-1.30   Drink and rest.

1.30-3.00   Bible Study 2.

3.00-3.15   Drink and rest.

3.15-3.45   The consequences of worry can be found in the following verses. Look up each Biblical reference and write down what can happen when we worry.

Matthew 13:22
Luke 21:34
Matthew 6:25-32

Now look up the following verses and see what happens when we have faith.

Acts 10:43
John 12:36
John 20:31
Ephesians 3:12
Romans 5:1
Acts 26:18

3.45-4.15 Read **Matthew 11:28-30**. Meditate on these verses and ask God to speak to you through them. Write down what he says and spend some time praying and resting/soaking in God.

4.15-4.30 Write down everything that concerns or worries you. Write down any stress situations that you find yourself in. Bring them before God one by one. Ask him to forgive you for any unbelief or lack of trust that you may have within you. Take time to give each situation or worry to God. Leave your burdens with God and thank him that his yoke is easy and his burden is light.

4.30-5.00 Spend an energetic time praising God. You cannot worry and praise at the same time. So having left your worries and concerns with God, spend time praising God for all He has done in you today and thank him that he is in control and is with you in all your problems.

BIBLE STUDY 1

Ephesians 1

Read the chapter at least three times.

1. Who wrote Ephesians?
2. When was it written?
3. Where was it written?
4. To whom was it written?
5. Write down a list of spiritual blessings we receive through Christ.
6. Read verse **4** again and make it personal, i.e. 'He chose me before....' Write down how that makes you feel.
7. What does Paul keep praying for the Ephesians?
8. Paraphrase verses **18-21**
9. Which verse speaks to you the most and why? Memorise that verse.
10. What is Paul trying to communicate through this chapter?

BIBLE STUDY 2

Ephesians 2

Read the chapter at least three times.

1. Who is Paul talking about when he mentions in verse **2** 'the ruler of the kingdom of the air'.
2. Verse **4** talks of God's great love for us. Find another verse in the Bible that talks of God's great love. Ask God to show you a picture of how great his love is for you. Spend a few minutes thanking him for his great love.
3. Meditate on verse **6**. Write down what you receive from God.
4. Memorise verses **8** and **9**.
5. Read verse **12**. There was a time when you did not know God and were *'without hope and without God in the world'*. Pray for two friends who are still in that position and ask God to speak to them.
6. With so much worry and stress in our world today, it's great to read verse **14**: *'For he himself is our peace'*. Take time to thank God for the peace he so freely gives us each and every day.
7. How many times is the word PEACE mentioned in this chapter?
8. This chapter talks a lot about us being *'fellow citizens with God's people and members of God's household'* (see verse **19**). How can we live in the world, but yet not be of this world?
9. What are the main things God has said to you through this chapter?

Nancy Goudie's
Spiritual Health Weekends

THREE EXCITING DAYS TO TRANSFORM YOUR SPIRITUAL WALK

Would you like to be pampered physically and toned up spiritually? Nancy Goudie's Spiritual Health Weekends could be just the thing you are looking for!

Nancy Goudie runs weekend conferences at the end of January and the beginning of February each year at luxury four-star Marriott Hotels in Preston and Bristol. These weekends are for ladies of all ages. Come and enjoy the excellent food, the superb leisure facilities *(spa, steam room, sauna, fitness room and luxury pool)*, the life changing sessions from Nancy, the magnificent banquet and 5 star entertainment and the free pamper treatments plus so much more. Each conference is usually booked well in advance so please book early to avoid disappointment.

This is a women's conference like no other!

FOR MORE INFORMATION AND BOOKING DETAILS CONTACT:

Zoe Wickham at   Tel: 01454 414880
ngm, Caedmon Complex,   Fax: 01454 414812
Bristol Road, Thornbury,   Email: zoewickham@ngm.org.uk
Bristol, BS35 3JA.   Or visit: www.nancygoudie.com

Other Books and Products
BY NANCY GOUDIE

HOT Faith - £5.00

If you want to find out about how ngm started or the amazing miracles that happened during their five year walk of faith to get their amazing missions and arts centre (Caedmon) then Nancy's book H.O.T. Faith (Hearing, Obeying, Trusting) is the book for you. It is a book filled with stories of faith exploits and will encourage you to walk by faith every day in life.

"Whatever mountains you need to move, this remarkable book will build your faith and empower your prayers."
Pete Greig 24/7 Prayer

Luv Esther - £3.00

This book takes you behind the scenes of the amazing luv esther musical. It's the story of how luv esther came about; how God provided more than half a million pounds and how God visited ngm with his deep intimacy. It is also a study on the life of Esther which can be used individually or in small groups.

"I throughly recommend this book to you."
Graham Kendrick

Treasures of Darkness - £5.00

This is a very naked and honest autobiographical account of a time when the world around Nancy started to collapse. Her husband Ray, fell into a dark pit where he experienced ill health and burnout. At the same time God was taking their ministry, ngm, through a shift, which caused much pain and insecurity and led to many people eventually leaving. Pressures swept in like a storm leaving devastation, confusion and unanswered prayers. Nancy discovered that through this time there were 'treasures of darkness and riches hidden in a secret place' (Isaiah 45:3).

The Beloved - £5.00
(hardback book)

This is a collection of real stories, poems, wise words, meditations and huge encouragement to know that you are God's beloved child. Any time you are feeling down, unloved, criticised or critical of yourself and life hits you hard, then pick up this book and flick through its pages. Each page is designed to bring you words of encouragement, hope and love.

Confident? - £5.00
(hardback book)

This book is for anyone who sometimes swings from being confident to feeling a failure. It's a book full of encouragement, wise words, poems, songs and stories to lift your spirit and get you back on your feet again, ready to face life once more. Through its pages you will feel accepted, really loved and realise afresh how amazing you are!

You are Special - £5.00
(hardback book)

In our culture of stress with so much pressure to look good and be famous, we often need to be reminded just how unique, precious, remarkable and extraordinary we are! No matter what colour our skin is, what size we are, what intelligence we display, what background we come from, the truth is each of us is an exceptional human being. In every page of this book you will discover the truth about yourself and realise afresh that you are deeply loved, special and accepted.

Oasis of Hope - £6.99
(hardback book)

There are times in our lives when we all need an oasis, a place where we can go and receive a thirst quenching drink for our souls. This book is such a place! A place where hope is renewed and faith can begin to grow. A place that will help refresh the reader physically, mentally, emotionally and spiritually. A place that gives us more of what we need to enable us to keep on going in our journey through life. It is designed to plant seeds of hope into the barren places of our hearts and encourage those seeds to grow and develop so that our faith will soar.

Oasis of Delight - £6.99
(hardback book)

There are times in our lives when we need an oasis, a place where we can go to receive a thirst quenching drink for our souls. This book is an exploration of what it means to live in the oasis of delight, tasting its fruit, relaxing and relishing in the lush surroundings; free to explore and enjoy the depths of his fulness of joy and his pleasures forevermore. It inspires us to enjoy the delightful fruit of intimacy with God whilst all the time pointing us towards the day when we will be in the ultimate garden of delight for eternity.

The Gift of Laughter - £6.00 (hardback book)

We live in an exhausting world often full of stress, concern and worry; one of the ways to help us navigate our way through life is laughter. Experts tell us that just 15 minutes of laughter can give the same benefit as two hours of sleep. It has been said that one good belly laugh burns of 3 to 4 calories and that laughing only 15 seconds can add two days to your life span! Each of us has been created with the ability to laugh. We already have the language of laughter within us and it has no negative side effects! Use it and it could increase our quality and even our quantity of life. If you are looking for tips, interesting quotes on laughter and many stories to help you laugh, then this is the book for you. These stories come from every day situations – some are funny and some are laugh out loud funny! You can open this book at any page and you fill find something either to make you laugh and giggle or something to encourage or inspire you to laugh out loud! This book is also available on Kindle.

All books are available direct from ngm on **www.ngm.org.uk/shop** or **www.nancygoudie.com** or through **www.amazon.co.uk**

MEDITATION CDS

Peace Like a River - £8.00

If you have ever experienced stress, carried worries, fought fears or are just looking for an oasis in your busy life, then this CD is for you. This recording will take you to a place of tranquillity where peace, love and grace are yours in abundance. Use this CD daily and you will find peace like a river flowing through your soul.

Smile - £8.00

If you are feeling the daily stresses of life, the busyness of work, the pressures of family or just need some soothing for your soul, then this recording is for you.

Meditations for the Beloved - £8.00

We all need to know we are loved and valued. This incredible music and meditation CD will take you to the secret place where you will know you are The Beloved; you will be overwhelmed with love, feel accepted and experience a peace that passes all understanding. This CD is also available to download from iTunes and other online platforms.

These CDs are suitable for those who are Christians and also those who are not and are available direct from ngm, Caedmon Complex, Bristol Road, Thornbury, Bristol, BS35 3JA, UK. Telephone – 01454 414880, **www.ngm.org.uk/shop** or through **www.amazon.co.uk**.

NEW GENERATION WORSHIP

Assured - £5.00
Assured is the debut EP from New Generation Worship featuring five fantastic new tracks. These new songs carry a fresh passion and prophetic edge. They all reflect a deep hunger for his presence which lies at the heart of the ngm community. Purchase this EP by visiting **www.ngm.org.uk/shop** or download from iTunes and other online platforms.

OTHER PRODUCTS

Nancy Goudie's Spiritual Health magazine - £2.75 (yearly)
Filled with stories, advice, tips and interesting articles – a great glossy magazine to brighten up your day!

Bible Reading Planners – 50p
A superb way of systematically reading through the Bible in one or two years. You can purchase these from ngm or through **www.nancygoudie.com**

Get in touch

Should you wish to contact Nancy then do write to her at:

ngm,
Caedmon Complex,
Bristol Road,
Thornbury,
Bristol, BS35 3JA,
UK.

Phone: 01454 414880
Email: nancy@nancygoudie.com
Website: www.nancygoudie.com

Follow Nancy on **twitter** (@NANCYGOUDIE)

Join 'Nancy Goudie's Spiritual Health Weekends' group on **facebook**.

Like Nancy Goudie page on **facebook**.
(www.facebook.com/nancygoudie)